THE BOOK OF THE PRESIDENTS

☆

VINCENT WILSON, JR.

Maps by
Peter Gui

American History Research Associates
Brookeville, Maryland

Printed in the United States of America
by
R. R. Donnelley & Sons Company
Crawfordsville, Indiana

ISBN 0-910086-02-8

Ninth Edition

American History Research Associates
Brookeville, Maryland

Contents

The Presidency

IN ALL history there has never been an office to compare with the Presidency of the United States. It stands alone—a monument to the political vision of the men who created it, an almost impossible challenge to the men who each generation seek it. In a world ruled by monarchs, a world where freedom was only a dream, against the background of an endless history of tyranny, the framers of the Constitution dared to create an experiment in freedom and a new kind of head of government to direct it; as Professor Clinton Rossiter has observed, they "took a momentous step when they fused the dignity of a king and the power of a prime minister in one elective office."

Although the broad limits of this office were defined in the Constitution, such niceties as whether to call the President "His Patriotic Majesty" or "His Highness the President," were debated by the nation's first Senators, so strong was the tradition of royal rule. More serious matters that concerned those Senators are still the subject of debate today, especially the extent of the powers granted the President under the Constitution; but, in the meantime, for the past 192 years, thirty-nine men have tried to meet the challenge of what has grown to be the most important office in the free world.

Throughout the history of the Republic the Presidency has been shaped by the men who held this high office; the strongest—Washington, Jefferson, Jackson, Lincoln, Wilson and the two Roosevelts* —have inevitably contributed most to its power and prestige. When Washington became President of the thirteen states, he brought the prestige of a great military commander *to* the new

---

* According to a 1948 poll of U.S. historians, who rated Theodore Roosevelt slightly below the other six. The poll did not cover President Truman, then in office.

office: he endowed it with a dignity and authority that not all his successors could command. As the country grew, so did the office of the President. Jefferson made it more democratic, less royal; and he established the Presidency as a political office that could effectively influence Congress. Jackson strengthened it by boldly exercising the full executive powers in dealing with both Congress and the states, powers that he felt the President drew directly from the people. And Lincoln, under the pressures of crisis and war, vastly extended the powers of the President and established a precedent followed by later war Presidents.

The peace-time powers of the President grew under Theodore Roosevelt, who identified his duty with a positive view of the President's role:

> I decline to adopt the view that what was imperatively necessary for the Nation could not be done by the President unless he could find some specific authorization to do it. My belief was that it was not only his right but his duty to do anything that the needs of the Nation demanded unless such action was forbidden by the Constitution or the laws.

Like Jackson, Theodore Roosevelt saw the President as the defender of all the people's interests, and in a growing industrial nation this meant an expansion of Presidential powers. With Wilson a new moral quality was brought to the office, a kind of executive responsibility that recognized the ascendancy of the United States as a world power and acknowledged the obligations of the President as one of the leaders of, and spokesmen for, all free men. Franklin Roosevelt carried this role even further by extending the domestic powers of the President and, as leader of the forces of the free world, by establishing the Presidency once again as a position of moral as well as political influence throughout the world.

The currents of history also had their effects upon the Presidency: the developments of science, the growth of American industry, and the continued westward expansion of the nation. George Washington presided over a country of approximately four million farmers, pioneers and shopkeepers thinly spread along the Eastern Seaboard, a country whose problems were simple enough to be handled by a few hundred Federal employees. But each of Washington's successors presided over a more complex country, one that expanded across the entire continent and at the same time was caught up in the greatest industrial and technological revolution the world has ever known, a country that now, as the leading industrial nation of the space age, requires over two million Federal employees to operate the many arms of government for its 224 million citizens. Inevitably the growth of the nation meant the growth of the executive powers; with the emergence of the U.S. as an industrial world power at the turn of the century, new responsibilities and new powers came, not to Congress, but to the Presidency. Recognizing this trend, Woodrow Wilson wrote in 1912: "The President can never again be the mere domestic figure he has been throughout so large a part of our history. The nation has risen to the first rank in power and resources. . . . Our President must always, henceforth, be one of the great powers of the world. . . ." Within the country, too, the powers of the Presidency increased with each new development in technology: the railroad, the airplane, radio and television have all brought the President closer to the people, the true source of his power, in spite of the fact that the population has increased fifty-fold since Washington's day.

Shaped both by past Presidents and by forces of history, the Presidency today challenges the capacities of the most gifted, the most dedicated of men. As the highest officer elected by *all* the people, the President must serve in place of a king as the Chief of State, the ceremonial head of the government who greets distinguished visitors, awards medals to heroes, and commemorates national events great and small. More important, he is the Chief Executive, directing the executive branch of the Government in its day-to-day operations; he is Chief Diplomat, directing the country's foreign relations; and he is Commander-in-Chief of all the nation's armed forces. Besides these specific duties he has many others: he proposes legislative programs to Congress; he serves as leader of his party; he is spokesman for the country and, at times, he assumes the position of moral leader for the entire free world. When it was a much smaller job, Washington complained of its demands; of the office in mid-twentieth century, Truman said, "No man can really fill the Presidency."

Beyond the almost overwhelming duties of the President is another burden, one that has made more than one President yearn to be a private citizen once again: the exposure to public criticism that each must endure. Since the founding of the Republic there have always been citizens—writers, cartoonists, editors—who were eager to exercise their freedom by taking the President to task on any issue, sometimes in the most immoderate terms. At the time that Washington was heralded as "The Father of His Country" he was also called "Step-father of His Country" and "An American Caesar," and accused of being "treacherous in private friendship and a hypocrite in public life." Abuse of the President and overzealous criticism of the Government during John Adams's administration—he was called a "despot" and burned in effigy—helped bring the restrictive Sedition Law into being, but Jefferson, who recognized that the law was unconstitutional, subjected himself to the most outrageous vilification. A Federalist cartoon depicted Jefferson as a drunken anarchist; campaign orators went so far as to question the legitimacy of his birth. Later Presidents fared little better: Jackson was mocked as "King Andrew"; Lincoln was called a "baboon," a "monster," and a "butcher," and threatened with flogging, hanging and burning at the stake, as well as the fate that was finally his. Johnson was castigated as a "drunkard," a "traitor," and a "faithless demagogue"; Theodore Roosevelt was labelled "The bloody hero of Kettle Hill"; Wilson a "despot"; and Franklin Roosevelt a "dictator" and "the paranoiac in the White House." With such excesses must each President live: among the rights the President is sworn to preserve is the right to speak *freely,* and most Presidents, while defending the principle, have been forced to suffer from the practice.

With awesome burdens and responsibilities, the Presidency has nonetheless continued to attract courageous and talented men. Why? Some of the answers may be found in the lives of the men who have sought and won that office, men whose lives have been as varied as the history of the country, men who were farmers, businessmen, journalists, lawyers, professors and generals. Spurred by ambition, by the will to serve, by the desire to contribute, each a focal point of the political forces of his time, the men who have served as President—no matter what they actually achieved—have each won a particular place in history as leaders of a unique experiment in democracy. Several proved to be liabilities to the Republic; some accomplished little; a few responded magnificently to grave challenges: but each of them contributed something—even if little more than continuity—to the greatest elective office in the world. The story of their lives is, after all, no less than the story of our country.

1st

GEORGE WASHINGTON

"Let us raise a standard to which the wise and honest can repair; the rest is in the hands of God."

—Address to the Constitutional Convention, 1787

To George Washington, as first President, fell the unprecedented task of organizing a national administration that was somehow to govern the thirteen separate states and yet preserve the freedoms for which the independent men of these states had so recently fought. It was his extraordinary task to make the radical idea of a government of free men, *by* free men, actually *work,* with nothing but the noble words of the freshly written Constitution to guide him. There were no existing buildings or departments, no procedures, precedents or traditions; there was no capitol. There was simply the Constitution and the man—and the mighty task.

Like other colonial landholders, Washington was a new kind of man in history—part cultivated gentleman, part rugged pioneer, a man in whom the ideas of Western civilization were combined with the great physical strength and fierce spirit of independence of the frontiersman. Among such men, Washington was outstanding. His performance as a surveyor and a soldier on the western frontier earned him, at 23, the command of Virginia's troops, and he served in the House of Burgesses for years before the Continental Congress chose him to lead the Continental Army. As its commander he held the struggling patriots together during the long war years; with victory, he quietly retired from the field. The presidential electors from the nearly sovereign states, cautious in selecting the man to hold power over *all* the states, had little to fear from one who had so willingly relinquished control of a victorious army.

Already the country's leading citizen, Washington carried out his duties as President with simple dignity. Although he tried to remain free of parties, he was closer to the Federalist Hamilton, his Secretary of the Treasury, than to the Democrat Jefferson, his Secretary of State. He firmly declined a third term, and spent his last years peacefully at Mount Vernon, where his tomb now stands. Of all memorials, the most dramatic is the graceful shaft of the monument in Washington, D. C., which symbolizes the aspirations of America as they were so nobly embodied in our first President.

THE UNITED STATES DURING WASHINGTON'S ADMINISTRATION

Population:

1790	3,929,214
1797	4,883,209

Key to Map:

- Existing States, 1789
- New States, 1789-97
- Existing Territories, 1789

SPANISH TERRITORY

SPANISH TERR.

BY GILBERT STUART — THE WHITE HOUSE COLLECTION

G° Washington

Born:
Westmoreland County, Virginia, February 22, 1732

Educated:
Common schools

Married:
Martha Dandridge Custis 1759

Career:
Surveyor in the western frontier 1748–
Officer with Virginia Forces 1752–
Commander-in-Chief of Virginia Forces 1755
Member of House of Burgesses 1759–74
Member of Continental Congress 1774–75
Commander-in-Chief of Continental Army 1775–83
Chairman of Constitutional Convention 1787–88
President 1789–97

Died:
Mount Vernon, Virginia, December 14, 1799

2nd

JOHN ADAMS

"Liberty cannot be preserved without a general knowledge among the people."

—DISSERTATION ON THE CANON AND FEUDAL LAW, 1765

IT WAS natural that Washington's Vice-President, John Adams, should succeed Washington, for in his own contentious but courageous way, he had contributed much to the new nation. Unlike Washington, Adams was not a great leader: he had neither a commanding nor a magnetic personality; he was a lawyer and an intellectual who made his greatest contributions before he became President. A man of bristling integrity, he could devote himself to a cause with a fierce intensity: he condemned the Stamp Act of 1765, was one of the first to support the idea of independence, and, at the Continental Congress when the colonies wavered before the mighty decision, he vigorously fought for acceptance of the Declaration of Independence. He further distinguished himself by representing the infant country with dignity—and success—in the leading courts of Europe.

By 1789 Adams was a respected but not a popular figure. In finishing second to Washington he received only 34 of 69 possible votes; and for eight years he was continually in the shadow of the commanding figure of Washington. Unfortunately his own term was little better: his struggle with Alexander Hamilton and his Cabinet members created factional strife in both the Federalist Party and the Government. Through the bitter disputes Adams remained essentially a Federalist, maintaining the strong central government established by Washington and Hamilton. When the Federalists passed the oppressive Alien and Sedition Laws in 1789, they assumed such sweeping powers over all critics of government that they challenged the essential freedoms of the individual; the party, already too closely allied with the propertied colonial aristocracy, carried the idea of a strong central government too far. Both Adams and the party lost favor: in the 1800 election Adams was defeated by Jefferson and the new Republican Party.

THE UNITED STATES DURING ADAMS'S ADMINISTRATION

POPULATION:

1797	4,883,209
1801	5,485,528

KEY TO MAP:

- Existing States, 1797
- Existing Territories, 1797

BY ASHER B. DURAND THE NEW-YORK HISTORICAL SOCIETY

John Adams

BORN:
Braintree, Massachusetts, October 30, 1735

EDUCATED:
Graduated from Harvard 1755

MARRIED:
Abigail Smith 1758

CAREER:
Lawyer 1758–
Member of Continental Congress 1774–78
Commissioner to France 1778
Drafted Massachusetts Constitution 1779
Minister to negotiate peace with England 1779
Minister to Netherlands 1780
Minister to England 1785
Vice-President 1789–97
President 1797–1801

DIED:
Quincy, Massachusetts, July 4, 1826

3rd

THOMAS JEFFERSON

"If there be any among us who would wish to dissolve this Union or to change its republican form, let them stand undisturbed as monuments of the safety with which error of opinion may be tolerated when reason is left free to combat it."

—INAUGURAL ADDRESS, 1801

CALLED the "Bloodless Revolution of 1800," Jefferson's election marked a profound but peaceful change in the administration of the young nation. The revolutionist who boldly wrote religious and ethical beliefs into the Declaration of Independence brought to the Presidency a philosophy of government firmly rooted in those same beliefs, a philosophy that concerned itself, above all, with the rights and liberties of the individual. It was Jefferson's democratic views, with his enduring faith in the individual, that, more than anything else, turned the country away from the class rule of the Federalists.

Few men have been better equipped to become President: a graduate of William and Mary College and an able lawyer, Jefferson helped shape the destiny of the struggling nation from the beginning—in the Virginia House of Burgesses, in the Continental Congress, and in the French court; and as Secretary of State under Washington and Vice-President under Adams.

As President, Jefferson demonstrated skillful political leadership by developing the growing Republican party, and through it, his influence in Congress; unlike Washington and Adams, he was undisputed head of his party—the first President to bring together the powers of the head of the party and of the state. And he proved to be a philosopher who practiced some of his "radical" principles; in the conduct of his office he had a fetish about equality: at official ceremonies he abandoned all distinctions of rank, as well as regal customs that had crept into earlier administrations. He brought a profound sense of democracy to the nation's highest office, an accomplishment that ranks with the celebrated purchase of the Louisiana Territory as an outstanding achievement of his administration.

A complex, brilliant man, Jefferson was one of the most accomplished of our Presidents: revolutionist, statesman, philosopher, architect, musician, inventor and writer, he was talented as are few men in any age—the living example of his own abiding belief in the capacity of the individual to learn and to grow—under freedom.

THE UNITED STATES DURING JEFFERSON'S ADMINISTRATION

POPULATION:

1801	5,485,528
1809	7,030,647

KEY TO MAP:

- Existing States, 1801
- New States, 1801-09
- Existing Territories, 1801
- New Territories, 1801-09

BY REMBRANDT PEALE THE NEW-YORK HISTORICAL SOCIETY

Th: Jefferson

Born:
Shadwell, Virginia, April 13, 1743

Educated:
Graduated from William and Mary College 1762

Married:
Martha Wayles Skelton 1772

Career:
Lawyer 1767–
Member of House of Burgesses 1769–74
Member of Continental Congress 1775–76
Member of Virginia House of Delegates 1776–79
Governor of Virginia 1779–81
Member of Continental Congress 1783–85
Minister to France 1785–89
Secretary of State 1790–93
Vice-President 1797–1801
President 1801–09
Founder of University of Virginia

Died:
Monticello, Virginia, July 4, 1826

4th

JAMES MADISON

"The public good, the real welfare of the great body of the people, is the supreme object to be pursued. . . ."

—The Federalist, 1788

A devoted disciple of Jefferson, Madison became the active leader of the Republican Party when he was elected President, but, though he held true to Jefferson's policies, he was never able to provide the kind of leadership that the Great Democrat brought to both offices. Like John Adams, Madison performed his greatest service to the nation before he was elected President: aware of the weaknesses of the confederation that loosely bound the states after the Revolution, he helped frame the Constitution in the Convention of 1787 and eloquently defended it in the Virginia ratifying convention and in the famed *Federalist* papers. And after the new government was formed, it was Madison who introduced the Bill of Rights to Congress as the first amendments to the Constitution.

The smallest man ever to become President, the soft-spoken, retiring Madison was more a scholar than an executive. He developed the habit of serious study at the College of New Jersey (Princeton) and became a devoted student of history and law. Besides the Constitution and the *Federalist* papers, other documents that helped shape the new nation can be traced to his pen: the petition for religious freedom in Virginia, the defense of U.S. navigation rights on the Mississippi, and the Virginia Resolution—a ringing denouncement of the oppressive Alien and Sedition Laws.

Foreign problems dominated Madison's years as President. Conflict with Britain over naval rights finally led to a war that brought little credit to either nation and made Madison the most unpopular President the country had thus far known. Federalists demanded that he resign, but he weathered the criticism; with peace he regained a measure of popularity. But nothing that he accomplished as President—or as member of Congress or Secretary of State—won him the high place he had already gained as one of the founders of the nation, a place of enduring fame as the Father of the Constitution.

THE UNITED STATES DURING MADISON'S ADMINISTRATION

Population:

1809 7,030,647
1817 8,898,892

Key to Map:

Existing States, 1809
New States, 1809-17
Existing Territories, 1809

SPANISH TERRITORY
SPANISH TERR.

BY ASHER B. DURAND — THE NEW-YORK HISTORICAL SOCIETY

Born:
Port Conway, Virginia, March 16, 1751

Educated:
Graduated from College of New Jersey (Princeton) 1771

Married:
Dolley Payne Todd 1794

Career:
Member of Virginia Constitutional Convention 1776
Member of Continental Congress 1780–83
Member of Constitutional Convention 1787
Member of Congress 1789–97
Secretary of State 1801–09
President 1809–17
Rector, University of Virginia 1826–36

Died:
Montpelier, Virginia, June 28, 1836

5th

JAMES MONROE

"The American continents . . . are henceforth not to be considered as subjects for future colonization by any European powers."

—MONROE DOCTRINE, 1823

THE first extended period of peace came to the young nation with Monroe's administration, the serene years known as the Era of Good Feeling. The European nations, exhausted by the Napoleonic wars, let the new nation develop in peace, and Monroe—and the U.S.—made the most of it: the U.S. persuaded Britain to agree to disarm forever along the Canadian border, purchased Florida from Spain, and asserted its growing authority by proclaiming the Monroe Doctrine—the warning to European nations against further conquest or colonization in the Western Hemisphere. At home the problem of slavery was temporarily solved by the Missouri Compromise, which admitted Missouri as a slave state but prohibited slavery north of the Mason-Dixon line.

Before reaching the Presidency, Monroe served in a variety of posts: he began as an eighteen-year-old Lieutenant in the Revolution; forty years later he held the unusual Cabinet position of Secretary of State and War. His long career was punctuated with controversy: as Washington's minister to France he earned Federalist disapproval and, finally, removal by his sympathy for the French cause; as Jefferson's minister to England, he concluded a treaty on naval problems that failed to uphold U.S. rights and was, therefore, rejected by Jefferson. However, as Jefferson's minister extraordinary in France he won a share of the credit for the purchase of Louisiana by signing the treaty that concluded the greatest of real estate transactions.

Monroe's administration brought to an end almost a quarter century of rule by the close friends that the Federalists called the Virginia Dynasty (Jefferson, Madison and Monroe). Like his friends, Monroe almost exhausted his fortune in a lifetime of public service; with them he helped block the Federalists' drift toward class rule and furthered the establishment of the government according to Jeffersonian principles of democracy.

THE UNITED STATES DURING MONROE'S ADMINISTRATION

POPULATION:

1817	8,898,892
1825	11,252,237

KEY TO MAP:

- Existing States, 1817
- New States, 1817-25
- Existing Territories, 1817
- New Territories, 1817-25

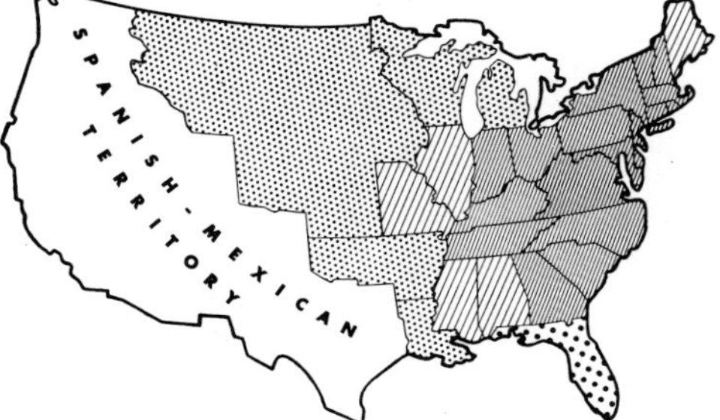

BY JOHN VANDERLYN — MELLON COLLECTION, NATIONAL GALLERY OF ART

James Monroe

Born:
Westmoreland County, Virginia, April 28, 1758

Educated:
Graduated from William and Mary College 1776

Married:
Elizabeth Kortright 1786

Career:
Continental Army 1776
Law student under Jefferson 1780–82
Member of Virginia House of Delegates 1782, 1787, 1810
U. S. Senator 1790–94
Minister to France 1794–96
Governor of Virginia 1799–1802; 1811
Special Minister to France 1803
Minister to England 1803–07
Secretary of State 1811–17
Secretary of War 1814–15
President 1817–25

Died:
New York City, July 4, 1831

6th

JOHN QUINCY ADAMS

"The great object of the institution of civil government is the improvement of the condition of those who are party to the social compact. . . ."

—Message to Congress, 1825

Monroe was the last of the Southern aristocrats of the Virginia Dynasty: the man who succeeded him was the last of the Northern aristocrats of the *Massachusetts* Dynasty—the Adams family of Braintree. For John Quincy Adams, though not born to the purple, was born to the red, white and blue. He literally grew up with the country: as a boy he watched the battle of Bunker Hill from a hill near home; at fourteen he served as secretary to the U.S. minister to Russia, at sixteen secretary at the treaty ending the Revolution. And he later held more offices than any earlier President.

The only son of a President ever to reach that office, John Quincy followed a career that closely resembled his father's: both attended Harvard, studied law, and were successful ministers and peace commissioners in Europe; both were elected President for only one term; both became involved in party conflicts and spent their least successful years in the White House.

Studious and crotchety, Adams was more successful as a diplomat and statesman than as a politician. As Monroe's Secretary of State he negotiated with the Spanish for Florida and was largely responsible for the document that became known as the Monroe Doctrine.

In the unusual election of 1824, four Democrat-Republicans contended for the Presidency. Andrew Jackson received almost 50,000 votes more than Adams, but less than the required majority. The decision thus rested with the House of Representatives, and when Henry Clay threw his support to Adams, the House elected John Quincy. Jackson felt cheated. The strong feeling that developed between Jackson and Adams ruined Adams's administration and finally drove the two men into separate parties—Adams the National Republicans, Jackson the Democrats.

Adams was more successful in Congress, where he served for his last seventeen years. There he distinguished himself by his dedicated fight to remove the "gag rule," which prevented Congress from considering any anti-slavery petitions. After fourteen years of struggle he finally won. But his service did not end until he collapsed on the floor of Congress in 1848, sixty-six years after he first served his country at his father's side.

THE UNITED STATES DURING ADAMS'S ADMINISTRATION

Population:

1825 11,252,237
1829 12,565,145

Key to Map:

Existing States, 1825
Existing Territories, 1825
Disputed Territory

MEXICAN TERRITORY

BY ASHER B. DURAND

THE CENTURY ASSOCIATION
COURTESY THE FRICK ART REFERENCE LIBRARY

John Quincy Adams

Born:
Braintree, Massachusetts, July 11, 1767

Educated:
Graduated from Harvard 1787

Married:
Louisa Catherine Johnson 1797

Career:
Secretary to U. S. Minister to Russia 1781
Lawyer 1791–
Minister to Netherlands 1794
Minister to Berlin 1797–1801
U. S. Senator 1803–08
Minister to Russia 1809–11
Peace Commissioner at Ghent 1814
Secretary of State 1817–25
President 1825–29
Member of Congress 1831–48

Died:
Washington, D. C., February 23, 1848

7th

ANDREW JACKSON

"There are no necessary evils in government. Its evils exist only in its abuses. If it would confine itself to equal protection, and, as Heaven does its rains, shower its favors alike on the high and low, the rich and poor, it would be an unqualified blessing."

—Veto of Bank Renewal Bill, 1832

Andrew Jackson was the first man of the people to become President; his election in 1828 stands in U.S. history as a great divide between government by aristocrats—the rich and well-born, as Hamilton described them—and government by leaders who were drawn from, and identified themselves with, the people. Under Jackson, Jefferson's democratic principles became more of a political reality, but Jackson had to reconcile those principles of political equality with the economic problems of an expanding industrial economy in a growing country. His election, like Jefferson's, marked a revolution in American democracy.

A child of the western frontier, Jackson was as rough-hewn as the log walls of his birthplace. From the time, at fourteen, when he fought in the Revolution, his life was largely one of struggle. On the frontier he studied law and gradually rose in Tennessee politics, representing the new state in Congress before he became state supreme court judge. But he gained fame not as a politician, but as a military hero. In the War of 1812 he commanded the U.S. forces that roundly defeated the British at New Orleans.

Tall, with a commanding presence, Jackson had a large, devoted personal following. And his stunning victory over John Quincy Adams in 1828 helped convince him that he was the champion of the people. With such a mandate he exercised his authority with a firm, and sometimes reckless, hand: he asserted the supremacy of the Federal government when South Carolina tried to nullify tariff laws, and, in his most dramatic act, he boldly vetoed the re-charter of the Bank of the United States, the half-private bank that had become powerful enough to threaten the Government itself. Jackson proclaimed that the Government should not "make the rich richer and the potent more powerful" at the expense of the rest of society.

The man who had been elected by a great popular majority—and had himself risen from the people—proved thirty years before Lincoln that American democracy could achieve government not only *of* and *for* the people, but *by* the people as well.

THE UNITED STATES DURING JACKSON'S ADMINISTRATION

Population:

1829 12,565,145

1837 15,843,452

Key to Map:

Existing States, 1829

New States, 1829-37

Existing Territories, 1829

Disputed Territory

BY RALPH E. W. EARL MELLON COLLECTION, NATIONAL GALLERY OF ART

Andrew Jackson

BORN:
Waxhaw, South Carolina, March 15, 1767

EDUCATED:
Self-educated

MARRIED:
Rachel Donelson Robards 1791

CAREER:
Messenger in Revolution 1780–81
Lawyer 1787–
Member of Congress 1796–97
U. S. Senator 1797–98
Justice of Tennessee Supreme Court 1798–1804
Major General, War of 1812
Commander of U. S. Forces, Seminole War, 1817–18
Governor of Florida Territory 1821
U. S. Senator 1823–25
President 1829–37

DIED:
Hermitage, Nashville, Tennessee, June 8, 1845

8th

MARTIN VAN BUREN

"From a small community we have risen to a people powerful in numbers and strength; but with our increase has gone hand in hand the progress of just principles."

—INAUGURAL ADDRESS, 1837

MARTIN VAN BUREN was America's first political boss. Elegant in dress, amiable and courteous in manner, "Little Van" early demonstrated such political skill that he rapidly rose to prominence in New York state politics: he became one of the leaders of the "Albany Regency," a political machine that developed a spoils system on a large scale and gained control of state politics in the 1820's. A masterful organizer, he welded diverse regional interests into the first effective national political party—the new Democrat party, which, in 1828, supported Andrew Jackson for the Presidency.

Coming to the Presidency after the fiery General, Van Buren inherited thorny financial problems; shortly after he took office, there were bread riots and banks failed—the country was caught up in the Panic of 1837. The skilled politician who had earned such names as "The Little Magician" and "The American Talleyrand" was unable to avert the financial upheaval, but he courageously attempted to improve matters. He established what later became the Treasury of the U.S., independent of any bank; but his administration was generally (and unfairly) held responsible for the Panic. He never regained his earlier popularity and was defeated by William Harrison in 1840. No more was the charming little gentleman in a snuff-colored coat seen gliding through the streets of Washington in an elegantly fitted coach attended by liveried footmen. Although he remained a national figure for many years, and was an unsuccessful Presidential candidate for the Free Soil Party in 1848, he spent most of his time in retirement at Lindenwald, his estate at Kinderhook, the quiet little village on the Hudson where he was born.

THE UNITED STATES DURING VAN BUREN'S ADMINISTRATION

POPULATION:

1837	15,843,452
1841	17,732,715

KEY TO MAP:

- Existing States, 1837
- Existing Territories, 1837
- Disputed Territory

MEXICAN TERRITORY

BY GEORGE P. A. HEALY — THE CORCORAN GALLERY OF ART

M. Van Buren

Born:
Kinderhook, New York, December 5, 1782

Educated:
Common schools

Married:
Hannah Hoes 1807

Career:
Lawyer 1803–
New York State Senator 1813–15
Attorney General of New York 1815–19
U. S. Senator 1821–29
Governor of New York 1829
Secretary of State 1829–31
Minister to England 1831–32
Vice-President 1833–37
President 1837–41

Died:
Kinderhook, New York, July 24, 1862

9th

WILLIAM H. HARRISON

"The only legitimate right to govern is an express grant of power from the governed."

—Inaugural Address, 1841

In 1840 the Whigs took the gamble of nominating the oldest man ever to run for President, 68-year-old William H. Harrison, and they won the election but lost the gamble, for Harrison lived only one month after his inauguration—the first President to die in office. He served the shortest term of any President, but his election ended the Jacksonian reign and brought the growing Whigs to power, even though John Tyler, the Vice-President who succeeded Harrison, was an ex-Democrat with rather watery Whig convictions.

The election of 1840 marked the beginning of elaborate national campaigns; by then the Whigs had become established as a second party, a development which helped to institutionalize the party system as the country's method of selecting candidates. Smarting from their defeat in 1836, when they were new and poorly organized, the Whigs met almost a year before the election for their first national convention. They then proceeded to build an elaborate campaign around everything but the issues: Harrison's military exploits against the Indians—especially the battle of Tippecanoe; and his service as a simple man of "The West"—the Ohio and Indiana Territories where he served as a civil and military leader. Campaign posters pictured Harrison as "The Hero of Tippecanoe" or "The Farmer of North Bend," hand to the plow in front of a log cabin. The catchy slogan "Tippecanoe and Tyler, too" rang out at the largest political rallies and mass meetings ever held in America. And it is one of the ironies of politics that the log cabin developed into a potent campaign symbol for Harrison, a man who was born in a white-pillared mansion into one of the aristocratic families of Tidewater Virginia. His father, Benjamin Harrison, was one of the Founding Fathers of the nation, a member of the Continental Congress and a signer of the Declaration of Independence.

THE UNITED STATES DURING HARRISON'S ADMINISTRATION

Population:

1841 17,732,715

Key to Map:

Existing States, 1841

Existing Territories, 1841

Disputed Territory

MEXICAN TERRITORY

BY E. F. ANDREWS THE CORCORAN GALLERY OF ART

W H Harrison

BORN:
Berkeley, Virginia, February 9, 1773

EDUCATED:
Graduated from Hampden-Sydney College 1790

MARRIED:
Anna Symmes 1795

CAREER:
Secretary of Northwest Territory 1798
Territorial Delegate to Congress 1799–1801
Govenor of Indiana Territory 1801–13
Commander of U. S. Forces in Northwest Territory 1811–12
Major General in War of 1812
Member of Congress from Ohio 1816–19
U. S. Senator 1825–28
Minister to Colombia 1828–29
President 1841

DIED:
Washington, D. C., April 4, 1841

10th

JOHN TYLER

"The institutions under which we live, my countrymen, secure each person in the perfect enjoyment of all his rights."

—INAUGURAL ADDRESS, 1841

JOHN TYLER, a tall Virginia gentleman, was the first Vice-President to complete the unexpired term of a President, but it is almost certain that the Whigs would never have chosen him as their Vice-Presidential candidate had they known he was to serve all but a month of Harrison's term. For by 1840 "Honest John" Tyler had clearly demonstrated that he was not a party man: during his years in Washington as a nominally Democratic Congressman and Senator he had followed such an independent course—fighting the Missouri Compromise, fighting high tariffs, fighting Jackson—that it finally led him, by 1833, out of the Democratic party altogether; yet his views on states' rights and on strict construction of the Constitution would never permit him to be at home with the Whigs. But the Whigs had nominated him, and, after Harrison's death, they had to live with him—as their Chief Executive.

It is not surprising that Tyler's years in the White House were tempestuous ones. When his stand on states' rights led him to veto a bill for a Bank of the United States, every member of Harrison's original Cabinet except Webster promptly resigned, and Webster, as Secretary of State, was at the time deeply involved in settling the northeastern boundary dispute with Great Britain. Tyler further alienated the Whigs by repudiating the spoils system and refusing to replace some Democratic ministers abroad. Throughout his term he was unable to work in harmony with the Whig majority in Congress, who were led by Henry Clay, the actual political leader of the party. They did agree with Tyler, however, on the annexation of Texas, which was accomplished in the final days of Tyler's term. But in the election of 1844 only an irregular Democratic convention nominated Tyler, and he withdrew before election. At a time when political parties were emerging as powers on the national political scene, John Tyler left the White House, a President without a party.

THE UNITED STATES DURING TYLER'S ADMINISTRATION

POPULATION:

1841	17,732,715
1845	20,181,683

KEY TO MAP:

- Existing States, 1841
- New States, 1841-45
- Existing Territories, 1841
- New Territories, 1841-45
- Disputed Territory

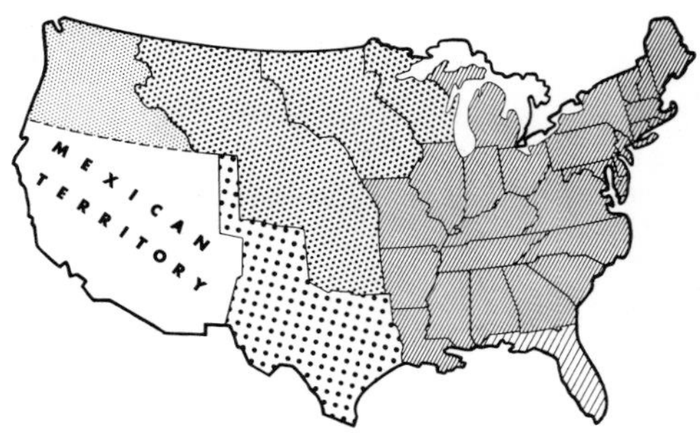

BY GEORGE P. A. HEALY

NATIONAL COLLECTION OF FINE ARTS, THE SMITHSONIAN INSTITUTION

John Tyler

Born:
Greenway, Virginia, March 29, 1790

Educated:
Graduated from William and Mary College 1807

Married:
Letitia Christian 1813 (Died 1842)
Julia Gardiner 1844

Career:
Lawyer 1809–
Member of Congress 1816–21
Member of Virginia Legislature 1823–25
Governor of Virginia 1825–26
U. S. Senator 1827–36
Vice-President March 4–April 4, 1841
President 1841–45
Member of Confederate Congress 1861–62

Died:
Richmond, Virginia, January 18, 1862

11th

JAMES K. POLK

"We must ever maintain the principle that the people of this continent alone have the right to decide their own destiny."

—MESSAGE TO CONGRESS, 1845

AN EXPANSIONIST mood dominated the country in the mid-1840's and the man who caught the spirit of the times and came from nowhere to lead the country through the period of its greatest expansion was James K. Polk of Tennessee. In spite of this distinction, Polk has been one of the most neglected of our Presidents. Emerging from comparative oblivion to become President, he has somehow managed to return there—in spite of a successful administration, one called by a leading historian ". . . the one bright spot in the dull void between Jackson and Lincoln."

When the delegates to the Democratic convention met in Baltimore in 1844, Polk was not even considered for the Presidency; before the convention was over he had become the first dark-horse candidate. And, in the election, when the Whigs made "Who Is Polk?" their battle cry, he answered them by soundly defeating their candidate Henry Clay, who was running in his third Presidential race.

As President the little-known Polk was a strong, though not radical, expansionist. During his administration the U.S. acquired the vast lands in the Southwest and Far West that extended the borders of the country almost to the present continental limits. Polk proved to be a forceful President in his direction of the Mexican War and in settling the Oregon boundary dispute with Great Britain; yet he did not yield to the extremists who wanted all of Mexico, nor to those who cried "Fifty-four forty or fight!" and claimed the Oregon Territory clear to the Alaskan border.

But the man who successfully led the country through its period of expansion strangely faded away when his work was done. Still popular at the end of his term but exhausted from overwork, Polk declined to be a candidate and returned to his home in Nashville, where he died at the age of 53—only three months after leaving the White House.

THE UNITED STATES DURING POLK'S ADMINISTRATION

POPULATION:

1845	20,181,683
1849	22,630,654

KEY TO MAP:

- Existing States, 1845
- New States, 1845-49
- Existing Territories, 1845
- New Territories, 1845-49

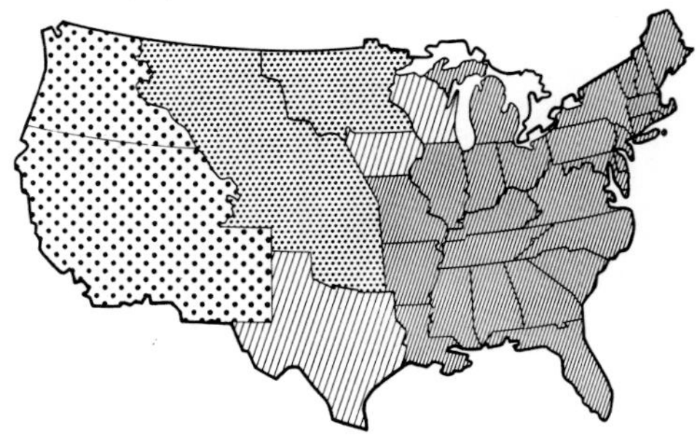

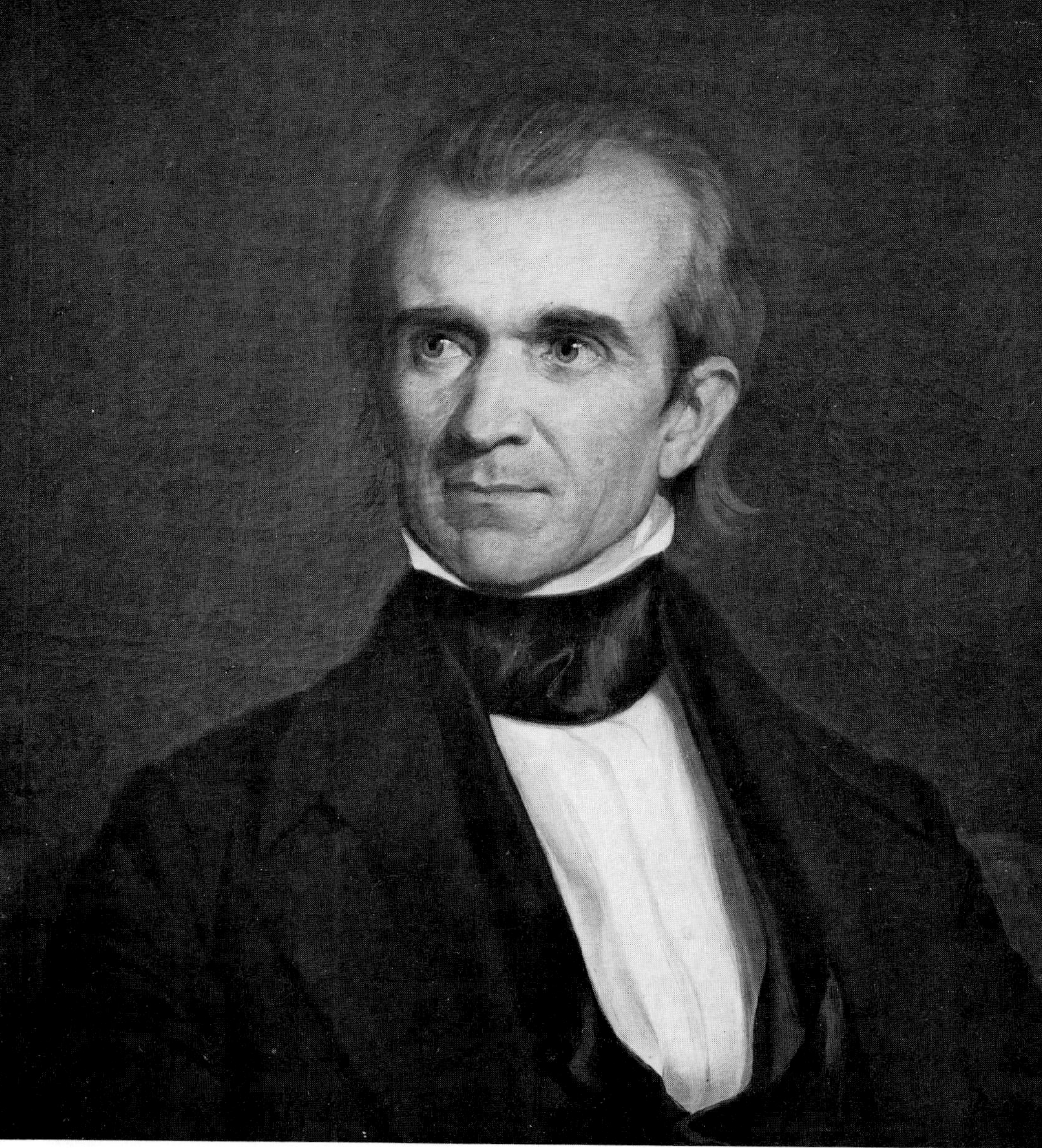

BY GEORGE P. A. HEALY THE CORCORAN GALLERY OF ART

Born:
Mecklenburg County, North Carolina, November 2, 1795

Educated:
Graduated from University of North Carolina 1818

Married:
Sarah Childress 1824

Career:
Lawyer 1820–
Member of Tennessee Legislature 1823–25
Member of Congress 1825–39
Speaker of the House 1835–39
Governor of Tennessee 1839–41
President 1845–49

Died:
Nashville, Tennessee, June 15, 1849

12th

ZACHARY TAYLOR

"For more than half a century . . . this Union has stood unshaken. . . . Whatever dangers may threaten it, I shall stand by it and maintain it in its integrity to the full extent of the obligations imposed and the powers conferred upon me by the Constitution."

—MESSAGE TO CONGRESS, 1849

TOBACCO-CHEWING General Taylor was the first Regular Army man to become President. It was solely on the strength of his popularity as a military hero that the Whigs chose him in 1848; never had a candidate known less about government, law or politics. "Old Rough and Ready" had practically no formal education, had spent his entire life moving from one Army post to another, and had never voted in an election in his life.

Although earlier Presidents had distinguished themselves in military service, none had made the Regular Army a career as Taylor did. Commissioned a First Lieutenant in the infantry in 1808, he served in almost every war and skirmish for the next forty years. As a young Captain in the War of 1812 he showed himself a cool and courageous leader; he won further recognition in the wars with the Black Hawks and Seminoles in later years. But it was his dramatic success in leading the American forces against the Mexican army in 1846-47 that caught the imagination of the American people and made him a national hero. In battle after battle he defeated the Mexicans—at Palo Alto, Reseca de la Palma and Monterrey—and then on February 22, 1847, he won his greatest victory at Buena Vista when his troops routed a large army led by General Santa Anna.

In the White House, Taylor saw his job as the civilian counterpart of a military commander; untutored in politics, he tried to remain nonpartisan, to leave legislative matters to Congress and simply execute the laws himself. But running the Government proved more complex: before long he became embroiled in the issue that haunted the country—slavery. Although unskilled in politics, he was a forthright and determined leader: when Southern Congressmen threatened trouble over the admission of California as a free state, Taylor, who owned slaves himself, warned that he would lead the Army against them and hang any who resisted as traitors. Thus the hero of the Mexican War, who died unexpectedly in July 1850, proved that, for all his lack of skill, he yet was able to take a stand on the issue the country dreaded facing. No successor until Lincoln was to show such courage.

THE UNITED STATES DURING TAYLOR'S ADMINISTRATION

POPULATION:

1849	22,630,654
1850	23,260,638

KEY TO MAP:

Existing States, 1849

Existing Territories, 1849

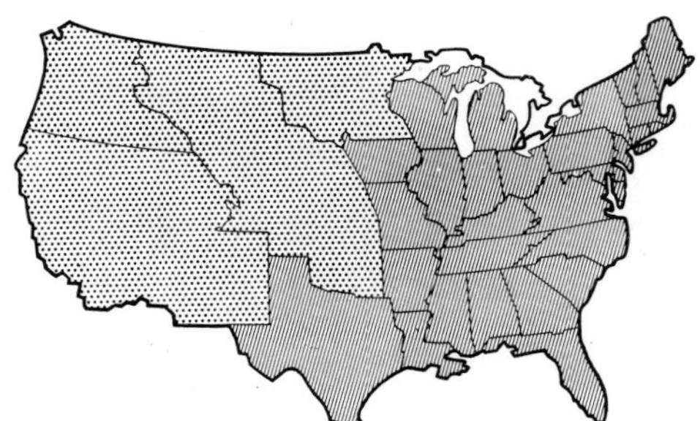

BY J. H. BUSH

THE WHITE HOUSE COLLECTION
COURTESY THE FRICK ART REFERENCE LIBRARY

Z. Taylor.

BORN:
Orange County, Virginia, November 24, 1784

EDUCATED:
Common schools

MARRIED:
Margaret Smith 1810

CAREER:
Lieutenant, U. S. Army 1808
Major in War of 1812
Colonel in Black Hawk War 1832
Brigadier General in Seminole War 1836–37
Major General in Mexican War 1845–47
President 1849–50

DIED:
Washington, D. C., July 9, 1850

13th

MILLARD FILLMORE

"I think no event would be hailed with more gratification by the people of the United States than the amicable adjustment of questions of difficulty which have now for a long time agitated the country. . . ."

—Message to Congress, 1850

When Vice-President Fillmore succeeded to the Presidency upon the death of Zachary Taylor, he became one of the select group of Presidents who have made the American myth "from a log cabin to the White House" a reality. But Fillmore's rise from humble apprentice to the highest office in the land was more inspiring than his performance in that office; however, he at least looked the part. When the short, stocky Taylor was still in the White House, Washingtonians observed that the tall, dignified Fillmore looked more like a president than the President himself.

Born in a log cabin in Cayuga County, New York, Fillmore overcame extreme handicaps: he had little formal education, worked on his father's farm, and at fifteen was apprenticed to a wool carder. While serving his apprenticeship he belatedly began his studies and gradually learned enough to teach school himself, so that he could afford to study law. At twenty-three he was admitted to the bar; by the time he was thirty he had established himself in Buffalo and won a seat in the New York State Assembly.

In politics Fillmore generally followed a moderate course, although in Congress he did espouse an unpopular cause by supporting John Q. Adams in his fight against the "gag rule" against anti-slavery bills. But as President he accepted Henry Clay's compromise measures on slavery and signed his political life away when he signed the Fugitive Slave Act. Part of the Compromise of 1850, the Act permitted slave owners to seize Negroes in the North as fugitives without process of law. The Act aroused extreme bitterness in the North; instead of improving conditions, it drove North and South ever farther apart. Although Fillmore could not then have realized it, his political career was practically over. The man who looked the part of a President was not even nominated by his own party to play the role again.

THE UNITED STATES DURING FILLMORE'S ADMINISTRATION

Population:

1850 23,260,638
1853 25,736,070

Key to Map:

Existing States, 1850

New States, 1850-53

Existing Territories, 1850

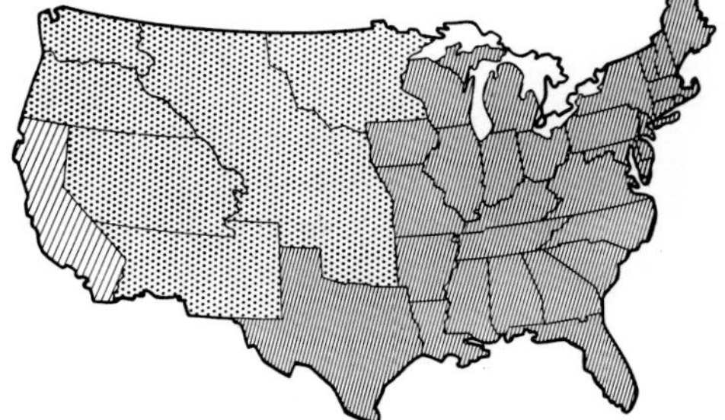

BY GEORGE P. A. HEALY THE CORCORAN GALLERY OF ART

Born:
Locke, New York, January 7, 1800

Educated:
Common school

Married:
Abigail Powers (Died 1853)
Caroline McIntosh

Career:
Lawyer 1823–
Member of New York Assembly 1828–31
Member of Congress 1833–35; 1837–45
Chancellor of University of Buffalo 1846–47
Comptroller of New York State 1847
Vice-President 1849–50
President 1850–53

Died:
Buffalo, New York, March 8, 1874

14th

FRANKLIN PIERCE

"In expressing briefly my views upon an important subject which has recently agitated the nation . . . , I fervently hope that the question is at rest and that no sectional or ambitious or fanatical excitement may again threaten the durability of our institutions. . . ."

—Inaugural Address, 1853

"I would rather be right than President," Henry Clay said, and he was often right but never President. But Franklin Pierce, a genial New Hampshire lawyer who said that the Presidency would be "utterly repugnant" to him, became our fourteenth President in spite of himself—without ever making a single campaign speech. Like Polk, Pierce had not even been considered a candidate before the Democratic convention, but he was reluctantly pushed into the role of compromise candidate when the convention reached a stalemate at the thirty-fifth ballot.

Although he served honorably in his state legislature and in the United States House and Senate, Pierce gradually developed a marked distaste for politics: in 1842 he resigned from the Senate to return to private practice, and later he refused several opportunities to return to office. Handsome, friendly Frank Pierce had retired from politics for life until he was caught up in the swirl of events that suddenly put him in the White House.

In 1853 slavery was still the dominant issue. Pierce took office with the belief that he should support the Compromise of 1850, and like Fillmore, he alienated the North by enforcing the Fugitive Slave Act. The Kansas-Nebraska Act, which created new territories in 1854, simply provided a new arena for the great struggle. In these new territories nothing was settled as abolitionists and pro-slavery groups resorted to force and bloodshed: "Bleeding Kansas" became an open wound.

On other fronts Pierce fared little better. Part of his expansionist policy was a plan to purchase Cuba, but he was forced to denounce three of his ministers (one, James Buchanan) when they declared in the Ostend Manifesto that the U.S. should *take* Cuba, if Spain refused to sell it. However, Pierce was able to purchase land from Mexico which gave us our present southwest border, completing our expansion in the West. Pierce was probably grateful when his party neglected to nominate him for another term. At last he could have his privacy.

THE UNITED STATES DURING PIERCE'S ADMINISTRATION

Population:

1853 25,736,070
1857 29,036,649

Key to Map:

Existing States, 1853
Existing Territories, 1853
New Territories, 1853-57

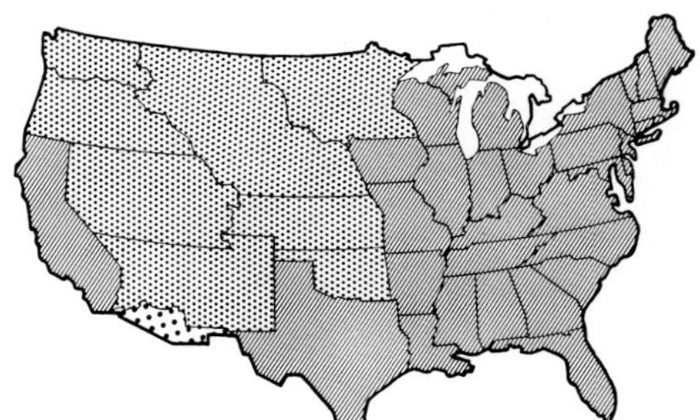

BY GEORGE P. A. HEALY — MELLON COLLECTION, NATIONAL GALLERY OF ART

Born:
Hillsboro, New Hampshire, November 23, 1804

Educated:
Graduated from Bowdoin College 1824

Married:
Jane Means Appleton 1834

Career:
Lawyer 1827–
Member of New Hampshire Legislature 1829–33
Member of Congress 1833–37
U. S. Senator 1837–42
Brigadier General in Mexican War 1847–48
President 1853–57

Died:
Concord, New Hampshire, October 8, 1869

15th

JAMES BUCHANAN

"Our Union rests upon public opinion, and can never be cemented by the blood of its citizens shed in civil war."

—MESSAGE TO CONGRESS, 1860

JAMES BUCHANAN has the distinction of being our only bachelor President. However, there was little distinctive about the administration of this man who followed the example of Fillmore and Pierce by futilely trying to satisfy both North and South. It is one of the ironies of fate—and of politics—that Buchanan, who was a brilliant young lawyer in the 1820's and a promising political figure in the 1830's, should have been passed over when he first sought the Presidential nomination in the 1840's, and finally selected to run only when he had become a tired, indecisive old man of 65, the second oldest President ever elected.

History has not dealt kindly with "Old Buck," whose record might have looked far better had he never reached the White House. His record as Congressman and Senator, as minister to Russia and Great Britain, and especially as Secretary of State under Polk, earned him a respectable though far from outstanding place in history. But he had the misfortune of reaching the nation's highest office well past his prime, at a time of impending crisis. And it was his further misfortune that the remedy of compromise that had in the past at least maintained a surface calm, was no longer sufficient; the problem had outgrown this kind of "solution": the test the nation had been avoiding almost since its beginning was upon it, and the old nostrums simply wouldn't work.

Unsure of himself, engrossed in legalistic details, Buchanan pursued a course which history has most dramatically demonstrated to be the wrong one. And it is his unhappy fate to be forever thrust into the shadows by the towering figure of his successor, the man who proved him wrong.

THE UNITED STATES DURING BUCHANAN'S ADMINISTRATION

POPULATION:

1857 29,036,649
1861 32,350,627

KEY TO MAP:

Existing States, 1857
New States, 1857-61
Existing Territories, 1857

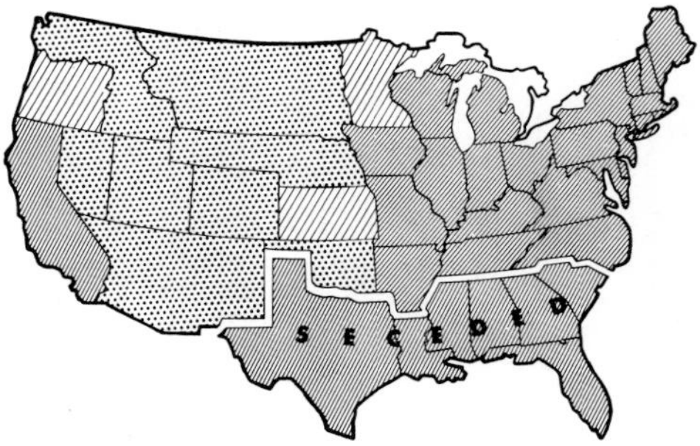

SECEDED

BY GEORGE P. A. HEALY — NATIONAL GALLERY OF ART

James Buchanan

Born:
Mercersburg, Pennsylvania, April 23, 1791

Educated:
Graduated from Dickinson College 1809

Never married

Career:
- Lawyer 1812–
- Member of Pennsylvania Legislature 1815–16
- Member of Congress 1821–31
- Minister to Russia 1832–34
- U. S. Senator 1834–45
- Secretary of State 1845–49
- Minister to Great Britain 1853–56
- President 1857–61

Died:
Lancaster, Pennsylvania, June 1, 1868

16th

ABRAHAM LINCOLN

"Why should there not be a patient confidence in the ultimate justice of the people? Is there any better or equal hope in the world?"

—INAUGURAL ADDRESS, 1861

IN ALL history there is no more dramatic example of the times calling forth a man equal to the challenge of a grave crisis than the legendary rise of Abraham Lincoln from obscurity to the Presidency of the crumbling Union. Every conceivable obstacle was there before him: humble birth, ignorance, poverty, and life in the wilderness of the frontier; he was completely without advantages or connections; he was too human ever to be a favorite of the professional politicians; he was too enigmatic, too philosophical, too humorous ever to be a great popular figure. But destiny was not to be thwarted: somehow Lincoln was nominated for the Presidency—as the second choice of many; and with less than a majority of the popular vote he managed to be elected in 1860.

Out of those early years of poverty and trial emerged a man uniquely suited to face the crisis of civil war—a man of haunting honesty, a man with a probing conscience and a penetrating intellect, a man of deep humanity. After the first eighteen months in office Lincoln became a strong, effective leader—firm, tactful, persuasive; but, above all, he proved to be a man of vision: he saw the United States in its largest dimension—as a noble experiment in democracy. In the long history of tyranny and oppression, here was man's great hope. To him the great ideal of democracy overshadowed regional differences. Lincoln's profound conviction of the enduring value of this experiment in free government sustained him throughout the long years of war; on the battlefield at Gettysburg it moved him to give the world a glimpse of his vision of the country's true greatness: "a nation conceived in liberty and dedicated to the proposition that all men are created equal," and of his ultimate reason for striving to preserve the Union: that "government of the people, by the people, and for the people shall not perish from the earth." One of the truly great political and human statements of all time, the Gettysburg Address reveals the sincerity, the simplicity and the essential nobility that mark Lincoln as one of our greatest Presidents.

THE UNITED STATES DURING LINCOLN'S ADMINISTRATION

POPULATION:

1861 32,350,627

1865 35,700,678

KEY TO MAP:

Existing States, 1861

New States, 1861-65

Existing Territories, 1861

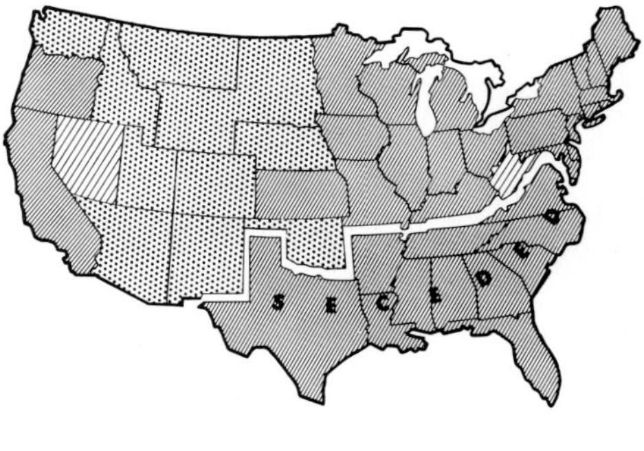

BY GEORGE P. A. HEALY MELLON COLLECTION, NATIONAL GALLERY OF ART

A. Lincoln

Born:
Hardin County, Kentucky, February 12, 1809

Educated:
Self-educated

Married:
Mary Todd 1842

Career:
Surveyor, Postmaster, Captain in Black Hawk War 1831–37
Member of Illinois Legislature 1834–42
Lawyer 1837–
Member of Congress 1847–49
President 1861–65

Died:
Washington, D. C., April 15, 1865

17th

ANDREW JOHNSON

"It is our sacred duty to transmit unimpaired to our posterity the blessings of liberty which were bequeathed to us by the founders of the Republic. . . ."

—MESSAGE TO CONGRESS, 1868

FEW men who have reached the Presidency have been less prepared for that high office than was Andrew Johnson. It is reported that he never spent a single day in a schoolroom. Bound as apprentice to a tailor when only a boy of ten, Johnson spent his youth working long hours in the shop. Only after he had established himself as a tailor in the mountain town of Greenville, Tennessee, and married Eliza McCardle, did he—with the help of his wife—make progress with his education. But, determined as he was, he never achieved the polish of the formally educated; unfortunately he also lacked the saving grace of the great human qualities of his predecessor.

But this rough-hewn politician who was plagued with political handicaps of background and personality yet left his mark on history, for through all his faults and failings shone the kind of integrity and courage that command universal respect. Never in sympathy with the Southern aristocracy, Johnson alone of the twenty-two Southern Senators refused to leave his senate seat in 1861 when his state seceded from the Union. Firm in his resolve, he served the Union as military Governor of Tennessee until he was elected Vice-President in 1864. And after Lincoln's death, the Presidency provided him further occasions for courageous action. Fighting the radical Republicans who wanted to grind the war-torn South under the Northern boot, Johnson fearlessly brought the wrath of the Republican Congress on his own head and narrowly missed impeachment—the only President ever to be involved in impeachment proceedings. But he survived that ordeal and, six years after leaving office, he had the pleasure of being elected once again to the Senate, where he had the opportunity to defend his own reconstruction policies before he died.

THE UNITED STATES DURING JOHNSON'S ADMINISTRATION

POPULATION:

1865	35,700,678
1869	39,050,729

KEY TO MAP:

- Existing States, 1865
- New States, 1865-69
- Existing Territories, 1865
- New Territories, 1865-69

BY E. F. ANDREWS THE CORCORAN GALLERY OF ART

Andrew Johnson

BORN:
Raleigh, North Carolina, December 29, 1808

EDUCATED:
Self-educated

MARRIED:
Eliza McCardle 1827

CAREER:
Tailor, Alderman 1826–
Mayor of Greenville 1830–33
Member of Tennessee Legislature 1835–43
Member of Congress 1843–53
Governor of Tennessee 1853–57
U. S. Senator 1857–62
Military Governor of Tennessee 1862–65
Vice-President March 4–April 15, 1865
President 1865–69
U. S. Senator 1875

DIED:
Carter's Depot, Tennessee, July 31, 1875

18th

ULYSSES S. GRANT

"I ask patient forbearance one toward another throughout the land, and a determined effort on the part of every citizen to do his share toward cementing a happy union. . . ."

—Inaugural Address, 1869

General Ulysses S. Grant was one of the nation's greatest military heroes but one of its most unsuccessful Presidents. Decisive and masterful on the battlefield, a dynamic leader and a horseman of great prowess, he proved to be ingenuous in the political arena. Raised on a farm, he early developed a love of horses and seemed always at his best on horseback.

As leader of the victorious forces of the North, Grant was considered the saviour of the Union. After Johnson's unhappy term, Republicans turned readily to Grant—even though he knew nothing about politics. Innocent and sincere, Grant committed errors of judgment from the beginning: he appointed two unknowns from his home town in Illinois to cabinet positions; and later he allowed himself to be entertained by two stock manipulators —Jay Gould and Jim Fisk—who tried to corner the gold market, a mistake which left him open to charges of incompetence and corruption. As the years passed, the evidences of corruption in his administration were such that Grant lost much of the popularity that first brought him into office. However, he managed to be re-elected to another term, one tarnished by even more corruption, more scandal.

In spite of the scandals, Grant scored a few victories. Passage of the Amnesty Bill in 1872 restored civil rights to most Southerners, relieving some of the harsh conditions of reconstruction. And, against considerable opposition, Grant took courageous steps to fight the growing threat of inflation. But the battle-torn country was still in distress; the General who had brought the great war to a successful close was not the man to bind up the nation's wounds.

THE UNITED STATES DURING GRANT'S ADMINISTRATION

Population:

1869 39,050,729
1877 47,140,727

Key to Map:

Existing States, 1869
New States, 1869-77
Existing Territories, 1869

BY THOMAS LE CLEAR

NATIONAL COLLECTION OF FINE ARTS,
THE SMITHSONIAN INSTITUTION

U. S. Grant

Born:
Point Pleasant, Ohio, April 27, 1822

Educated:
Graduated from West Point 1843

Married:
Julia Dent 1848

Career:
Captain, U. S. Army in Mexican War 1846–48
U. S. Army Officer in Oregon and California 1848–54
Farmer, real estate dealer, clerk 1854–61
Brigadier General—General in Civil War 1861–65
President 1869–77
Partner in brokerage firm in New York 1880–84

Died:
New York City, July 23, 1885

19th

RUTHERFORD B. HAYES

"He serves his party best who serves his country best."
—INAUGURAL ADDRESS, 1877

AFTER the scandals of Grant's administration the Republicans wanted an especially upright candidate; they found him in Rutherford B. Hayes, a devout, conscientious Ohioan whose Puritan ancestors had come from New England. In his third term as Governor of Ohio in 1876, Hayes was known for his honest administration, his constructive reforms, and his stand on sound money—one of the leading issues of the day. In addition, he had an outstanding military record: with the Ohio Volunteers he had performed with gallantry and emerged a Major General. He was above reproach.

Yet it is one of the quirks of history that such a man as Hayes should reach the White House through a very questionable settlement of a disputed election, although it is generally agreed that Hayes himself was not at all involved. The settlement was in the hands of a special electoral commission that happened to have a majority of Republicans.

But the Republicans had chosen well—better than some of them knew. For President Hayes proved to be too honest and forthright for many of them, who could hardly wait to get him out of office. Despite political undercurrents, Hayes made good use of his one term to stabilize the Government on several fronts. He reduced post-war bitterness by withdrawing Federal troops from Southern states; he established reforms in civil service; he took courageous steps to settle the railroad strike of 1877; and he stood firm in enforcing a sound money policy—all in the face of vigorous opposition.

The man chosen to remove the taint of scandal from the Government proved to be surprisingly resolute and effective; his dedication to principle and his courageous and forthright actions won him the kind of praise earned by few one-term Presidents.

THE UNITED STATES DURING HAYES'S ADMINISTRATION

POPULATION:

1877	47,140,727
1881	51,541,575

KEY TO MAP:

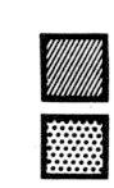

Existing States, 1877

Existing Territories, 1877

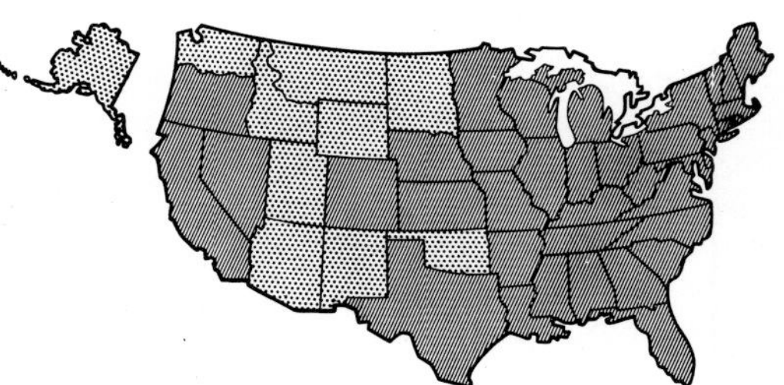

BY DANIEL HUNTINGTON

THE WHITE HOUSE COLLECTION
COURTESY THE FRICK ART REFERENCE LIBRARY

R. B. Hayes

Born:
Delaware, Ohio, October 4, 1822

Educated:
Graduated from Kenyon College 1842; Harvard Law School 1845

Married:
Lucy Webb 1852

Career:
Lawyer 1845–
City Attorney of Cincinnati 1858–60
Officer in Civil War 1861–65 (Major General 1864–)
Member of Congress 1865–67
Governor of Ohio 1868–72; 1876–77
President 1877–81

Died:
Fremont, Ohio, January 17, 1893

20th

JAMES A. GARFIELD

"Next in importance to freedom and justice is popular education, without which neither freedom nor justice can be permanently maintained."

—LETTER ACCEPTING PRESIDENTIAL NOMINATION, 1880

GARFIELD was the last of the Presidents to go from a log cabin to the White House. Left fatherless when only an infant, he was forced to work from his earliest years on the family farm in Orange, Ohio. Besides helping his widowed mother, he also succeeded in earning enough—as a canal boat driver, carpenter, and teacher—to put himself through college. His love of learning led him from Hiram Institute in Ohio to Williams College, and then back to Hiram, where he became professor of Latin and Greek and later president.

The same drive that brought Garfield into the scholarly ranks carried him into public life. In northern Ohio he became known as a powerful anti-slavery speaker and grew active in politics. A brilliant career in the Army—a Brigadier General at thirty—was interrupted when he resigned after being elected to Congress. There he served for eighteen years, emerging in 1880 as a leader of his party.

But when the Republicans met in Chicago in 1880, Garfield was not considered a contender. The struggle was between Grant, who was willing to try a third term, and Senator James G. Blaine of Maine, but as happened before, the convention was so divided that neither could win. Finally, on the thirty-sixth ballot, the dark-horse Garfield was nominated.

The surprise gift of the highest office in the land was not one that Garfield enjoyed for long. In the White House he showed signs of being a strong executive, independent of party as was Hayes. But he was in office less than four months when he was fatally shot by a crazed office seeker as he was about to catch a train in the Washington depot. Like that earlier log-cabin President, Garfield left the White House a martyr, having spent less time in office than any President except Harrison.

THE UNITED STATES DURING GARFIELD'S ADMINISTRATION

POPULATION:

1881 51,541,575

KEY TO MAP:

Existing States, 1881

Existing Territories, 1881

BY CALVIN CURTIS

THE WHITE HOUSE COLLECTION
COURTESY THE FRICK ART REFERENCE LIBRARY

J. A. Garfield.

Born:
Orange, Ohio, November 19, 1831

Educated:
Graduated from Williams College 1856

Married:
Lucretia Rudolph 1858

Career:
Professor of Latin and Greek at Hiram Institute, Ohio 1856–57
President of Hiram Institute 1857–61
Member of Ohio Legislature 1859–61
Officer in Civil War 1861–63 (Major General 1863)
Member of Congress 1863–80
U. S. Senator 1880
President 1881

Died:
Elberon, New Jersey, September 19, 1881

CHESTER A. ARTHUR

"No higher or more assuring proof could exist of the strength and permanence of popular government than the fact that though the chosen of the people be struck down, his constitutional successor is peacefully installed without shock or strain. . . ."

—Inaugural Address, 1881

Although the nomination and election of the dark-horse Garfield surprised many Americans, the nomination of Chester Arthur as Vice-President was a real shock, and many a citizen feared the worst when Garfield died in September 1881 with three and a half years of his term remaining. There was reason for the public to be worried: Arthur, who loved fine clothes and elegant living, had been associated with the corrupt New York Republican machine for almost twenty years, and, although the degree of his involvement had been difficult to establish, in 1878 he was finally removed from his post as Collector of the Port of New York by President Hayes, who had become alarmed at the misuse of patronage. But in spite of his questionable record, Arthur was nominated Vice-President—largely to appease Senator Roscoe Conkling and his powerful New York machine. Thus, when Arthur became President, there was every expectation that the free-wheeling spoils system that had reigned in New York would be firmly established in Washington.

But Chester Arthur fooled everyone—friends and enemies alike: somehow the responsibilities of that high office turned this petty politician into a man sincerely dedicated to the good of the country. Courageously he established his independence by vetoing a graft-laden rivers-and-harbors bill, by breaking with his former boss Conkling, and by vigorously prosecuting members of his own party accused of defrauding the Government. And, most important, instead of a spoils system, he supported a Federal Civil Service based on competitive examinations and a non-political merit system.

By his courageous acts Arthur won over many who had first feared his coming to power, but he lost the support of the political bosses. Although he was not an inspiring leader of men, he earned the nation's gratitude as the champion of the Civil Service system.

THE UNITED STATES DURING ARTHUR'S ADMINISTRATION

Population:

1881	51,541,575
1885	56,658,347

Key to Map:

Existing States, 1881

Existing Territories, 1881

BY GEORGE P. A. HEALY THE CORCORAN GALLERY OF ART

C. A. Arthur

Born:
Fairfield, Vermont, October 5, 1830

Educated:
Graduated from Union College 1848

Married:
Ellen Lewis Herndon 1859

Career:
School teacher in Vermont 1851–53
Lawyer 1853–
Quartermaster General of New York State 1861–65
Collector of the Port of New York 1871–78
Vice-President March 4–September 19, 1881
President 1881–85

Died:
New York City, November 18, 1886

22nd, 24th

GROVER CLEVELAND

"Your every voter, as surely as your chief magistrate, exercises a public trust."

—Inaugural Address, 1885

Grover Cleveland is a fine example of an American citizen whose crusading spirit carried him all the way to the White House—in spite of strong opposition from *both* parties—and, after he had been defeated, it carried him to office once again—the only President ever to succeed his successor.

With a limited formal education, Cleveland managed to study law and establish himself as a scrupulously honest office-holder in Buffalo and western New York state. By 1882 his reputation as a dedicated and effective administrator won him the Governorship of New York, a post in which he gained further renown by fighting the New York City Democratic machine. "We love him for the enemies he has made," said the delegate nominating Cleveland for the Presidency at the 1884 Democratic convention, for Grover the Crusader had not hesitated to stamp out corruption in his own party. To many of both parties he was the incarnation of clean, honest government. After the stains of the reconstruction era, it was time for a change: "Grover the Good" was elected in 1884, the first Democratic President in twenty-four years.

In office Cleveland was a doer—and he continued to make enemies: he made civil service reform a reality by courageously placing a number of political jobs under the protection of civil service, and he stood firmly against a high protective tariff, moves that contributed to his defeat in 1888.

While out of office Cleveland assumed the role of party spokesman and became an active critic of the Harrison administration. In 1892 he soundly defeated the man who had replaced him in the White House. But he returned to power in grim times with a depression cutting deep into the nation's economy; strong measures were called for, and in forcing repeal of silver legislation and halting the Pullman labor strike, Cleveland demonstrated a firm hand. Throughout a difficult term he remained an honest, independent leader, a man who left office with the hard-won respect of members of both parties.

THE UNITED STATES DURING CLEVELAND'S ADMINISTRATIONS

Population:

Year	Population
1885	56,658,347
1889	61,775,121
1893	66,970,496
1897	72,189,240

Key to Map (Second Administration):

- Existing States, 1893
- New States, 1893-97
- Existing Territories, 1893

BY HASSACK THE NEW-YORK HISTORICAL SOCIETY

BORN:
Caldwell, New Jersey, March 18, 1837

EDUCATED:
Common school

MARRIED:
Frances Folsom 1886

CAREER:
Lawyer 1859–
Assistant District Attorney of Erie County, New York 1863–65
Sheriff of Erie County 1870–73
Mayor of Buffalo 1882
Governor of New York 1883–85
President 1885–89; 1893–97

DIED:
Princeton, New Jersey, June 24, 1908

23rd

BENJAMIN HARRISON

"Let those who would die for the flag on the field of battle give a better proof of their patriotism and a higher glory to their country by promoting fraternity and justice."

—Inaugural Address, 1889

Grandson of a President and great-grandson of a signer of the Declaration of Independence, Benjamin Harrison carried a distinguished American name into the White House, but historians generally agree that he added very little distinction to it during his stay there.

Harrison's early years were filled with promise and success: admitted to the Indiana bar at the age of twenty, he became one of the state's ablest lawyers, and he interrupted his law career only to become a thirty-two-year-old Brigadier General in the Civil War. But the success that marked his early years deserted him when he entered politics after the war. Shortly after returning to Indiana he was defeated running for governor. After one term in the U. S. Senate he failed to be re-elected in 1887. And his victory over Cleveland in the Presidential election of 1888 was matched by a defeat at his hands when the two ran against each other in 1892.

Although he performed bravely on the battlefield, Harrison was not a bold President. Strongly supported and influenced by the mammoth trusts and other business interests, he signed into law one of the highest protective tariffs the country has ever known; and even when a bill to curb the trusts—the Sherman Anti-Trust Act—managed to be passed, his administration did little to enforce it. In spite of such concessions to business, the times grew worse. Harrison permitted the country's gold reserves to be severely depleted by a questionable Civil-War pension plan. By the close of his administration the signs of depression had multiplied: what was good for the trusts had not proved to be good for the nation. The cautious man who was afraid of the new electric lights in the White House had failed to convince the country that he could lead on to better times: once again the country turned to Cleveland.

THE UNITED STATES DURING HARRISON'S ADMINISTRATION

Population:

1889 61,775,121
1893 66,970,496

Key to Map:

Existing States, 1889
New States, 1889-93
Existing Territories, 1889

BY WILLIAM T. MATHEWS THE CORCORAN GALLERY OF ART

Benj Harrison

BORN:
North Bend, Ohio, August 20, 1833

EDUCATED:
Graduated Miami University, Ohio 1852

MARRIED:
Caroline Scott 1853 (Died 1892)
Mary Dimmick 1896

CAREER:
Lawyer 1853–
City Attorney, Indianapolis 1857–61
Reporter, Indiana Supreme Court 1861–62
Officer in Civil War 1862–65 (Brigadier General 1865)
U. S. Senator 1881–87
President 1889–93

DIED:
Indianapolis, Indiana, March 13, 1901

25th

WILLIAM McKINLEY

"We want no war of conquest. . . . War should never be entered upon until every agency of peace has failed."

—Inaugural Address, 1897

Although McKinley was a kind, gentle man beloved by many Americans, he did *not* earn a place in history as a champion of the people: his administration was closely identified with the trusts and special interests. At a time when the expanding West and the agrarian South were developing a people's movement of growing political significance, the dignified lawyer from Canton, Ohio, represented the bankers and industrialists who formed a powerful bloc in the Republican Party.

Both economically and politically, McKinley was a conservative; on the three burning issues of the day—the tariff, currency, and Cuba—he took a conservative position. The McKinley Tariff Bill, passed in 1890, was one of the highest protective tariffs in U. S. history. As President, McKinley supported the gold standard and for a time resisted those who wanted to stampede the U. S. into war with Spain to rescue an oppressed Cuba.

McKinley had been elected on a platform supporting Cuban independence. American investments in sugar plantations and trade with Cuba were at stake, and U. S. newspapers kept stories of Spanish atrocities in Cuba before the eyes of the public; the pressure for U. S. intervention—after the sinking of the U. S. battleship *Maine* in Havana harbor—finally moved McKinley to go to war despite cries of "Imperialism." When the victorious U. S. was given Puerto Rico and the Philippines, the cries of "Imperialism" grew louder. Ironically, the conservative McKinley launched the U. S. as a global power.

With McKinley's re-election in 1900 big business seemed secure for four more years. But a series of accidents dramatically altered this serene picture. In the 1900 campaign the progressive Governor of New York, Theodore Roosevelt, was put on the ticket as Vice-President by rival New York Republican leaders who hoped that post would be his political graveyard. But only six months after the inauguration McKinley was fatally shot by an anarchist at the Pan-American Exposition in Buffalo. And the era of free-wheeling big business died with McKinley, the third martyred President.

THE UNITED STATES DURING McKINLEY'S ADMINISTRATION

Population:

1897 72,189,240
1901 77,585,000

Key to Map:

Existing States, 1897

Existing Territories, 1897

New Territories, 1897-1901

BY H. T. SEE THE NEW-YORK HISTORICAL SOCIETY

Wm McKinley

BORN:
Niles, Ohio, January 29, 1843

EDUCATED:
Attended Allegheny College 1860

CAREER:
Soldier, Officer in Civil War 1861–65 (Major 1865)
Lawyer 1867–
Member of Congress 1877–91
Governor of Ohio 1892–96
President 1897–1901

MARRIED:
Ida Saxton 1871

DIED:
Buffalo, New York, September 14, 1901

26th

THEODORE ROOSEVELT

"It is well indeed for our land that we of this generation have learned to think nationally."

—BUILDERS OF THE STATE

THEODORE ROOSEVELT was the first progressive, the first modern President. A reformer and fighter, he was the most colorful and the most controversial President since Lincoln, the most versatile since Jefferson.

Born to wealth, Roosevelt was imbued with a strong sense of public service; in every position he held—from New York Police Commissioner to President—he fought for improvement and reform. His was largely a moral crusade: he saw his chief enemy as human weakness and corruption, and he vigorously fought it wherever he found it—in business or in government.

In the White House the many-sided personality of Roosevelt captured the American imagination. The youngest man to become President, this dynamic reformer who combined a Harvard accent with the toughness of a Dakota cowboy was a totally new kind of President. Fighting the "malefactors of great wealth," Roosevelt struck out against the mammoth trusts that appeared to be outside of Government regulation. The railroads, the food and drug industries, and enterprises using the natural wealth of the public lands all were subjected to some form of regulation, for the protection of the public interest. Many conservation practices began with Roosevelt.

A reformer at home, he was an avowed expansionist abroad. He supported the Spanish War and led his "Rough Riders" to fame; when President, he acquired the Canal Zone from Panama and sent U. S. battleships on a world cruise—to show off America's growing strength.

Perhaps most notable were Roosevelt's efforts to end the Russo-Japanese War, an achievement that won him the Nobel Peace Prize. But this peacemaker, soldier, explorer, hunter, scientist, writer and progressive statesman left many a mark upon history: to government he brought the fresh winds of reform, and the courage, vigor and tenacity to make his reforms an enduring part of the American scene.

THE UNITED STATES DURING ROOSEVELT'S ADMINISTRATION

POPULATION:

1901 77,585,000
1909 90,492,000

KEY TO MAP:

Existing States, 1901
New States, 1901–09
Existing Territories, 1901

BY G. B. TORREY — THE UNION LEAGUE CLUB, NEW YORK

Theodore Roosevelt

Born:
New York City, October 27, 1858

Educated:
Graduated from Harvard 1880

Married:
Alice H. Lee 1880 (Died 1884)
Edith Kermit Carow 1886

Career:
Member of New York Assembly 1882-84
Rancher, North Dakota 1884-86
Member of U.S. Civil Service Commission 1889-95
President of New York City Police Board 1895-97
Assistant Secretary of the Navy 1897-98
Colonel of Rough Riders 1898
Governor of New York 1898-1900
Vice-President March 4-September 14, 1901
President 1901-09
Leader of Expeditions in Africa (1909-10) and South America (1913-14)

Died:
Long Island, New York, January 6, 1919

27th

WILLIAM H. TAFT

"A government is for the benefit of all the people. . . ."
—Veto of Arizona Enabling Act, 1911

William Howard Taft was the country's largest President, a jovial, warm-hearted mountain of a man with a brilliant legal mind—an excellent administrator but a poor politician. He served with distinction as the first governor of the Philippines and as Roosevelt's Secretary of War, positions in which his amiable nature served to advantage.

But it was Taft's great misfortune to succeed such a dazzling political figure as Roosevelt in the Presidency and attempt to carry out his many new policies. Probably no successor could have pleased Roosevelt, but the fall from grace of the devoted friend Roosevelt had practically placed in the White House is one of the most tragic affairs in the history of the Presidency. Near the end of Taft's administration, when it was clear that he had not completely supported Roosevelt's Square Deal and had made concessions to the conservatives, Roosevelt fiercely attacked him in speeches and articles. In the 1912 election Roosevelt organized a progressive "Bull Moose" party and, running against Taft and the Republican Party—as well as the Democrat Woodrow Wilson—took enough votes from Taft to deprive either of victory, although their combined votes totaled over a million more than Wilson's.

In spite of the rift with Roosevelt, Taft continued to serve his country. After teaching law at Yale he was appointed by President Harding to the post that he had long sought, one that probably meant more to him than the Presidency: in 1921 he became Chief Justice of the Supreme Court, the only man ever to hold both offices.

THE UNITED STATES DURING TAFT'S ADMINISTRATION

Population:

1909	90,492,000
1913	97,227,000

Key to Map:

Existing States, 1909

New States, 1909-13

Existing Territories, 1909

BY A. L. ZORN

THE WHITE HOUSE COLLECTION
COURTESY THE FRICK ART REFERENCE LIBRARY

Wm H Taft

Born:
Cincinnati, Ohio, September 15, 1857

Educated:
Graduated from Yale 1878

Married:
Helen Herron 1886

Career:
Lawyer 1880–
Judge, Ohio Superior Court 1887–90
U. S. Solicitor General 1890–92
U. S. Circuit Court Judge 1892–1900
Governor of the Philippines 1901–04
Secretary of War 1904–08
President 1909–13
Professor of Law at Yale 1913–21
Chief Justice of the U. S. Supreme Court 1921–30

Died:
Washington, D. C., March 8, 1930

28th

WOODROW WILSON

"There must be, not a balance of power, but a community of power; not organized rivalries, but an organized common peace."

—Address to the Senate, 1917

Scholar, historian and reformer, Woodrow Wilson brought to the White House a highly developed idea of the role of the President as a moral as well as political leader of the nation. It was his philosophy that the President should actively *lead* the country by proposing constructive legislation to Congress. And he immediately put this philosophy into practice by delivering his first message to Congress himself, the first President to go to the Capitol since John Adams.

Although Wilson held only one political office before he became President, his years as a professor of history provided him with a detailed knowledge of political processes; as president of Princeton University and governor of New Jersey he proved himself an able, dedicated administrator, unafraid to institute reforms. Thus Wilson's philosophy, knowledge and ability uniquely equipped him for the nation's highest office.

Wilson's first energies were directed toward domestic issues: a lower tariff, stronger anti-trust measures, a child-labor law, the first income-tax law, and the Federal Reserve Act—the last greatly improving the government's control of money. But the country that had emerged as a world power under McKinley and Roosevelt could not long ignore the conflict in Europe. Wilson kept the U.S. out of war during his first term, but America's sympathy with the Allies and Germany's aggressive submarine warfare made the U.S.'s "neutral" posture difficult to maintain. "To make the world safe for democracy," Wilson finally led the nation into war in 1917.

In directing the war effort Wilson cooperated with a Congress that gave him vast emergency powers. While mobilizing the industrial as well as the military forces of the nation, he labored over plans for peace: his great hope was the League of Nations. But his dedication to the noble ideal of the League's Covenant led to a bitter conflict with Congress when the Covenant, already signed by the European powers, was before them for approval. When Congress rejected it, he suffered his greatest defeat, but it was not a total one, for he had given to the world the powerful idea of uniting the great moral and political forces of world opinion, a principle that lives on in the United Nations.

THE UNITED STATES DURING WILSON'S ADMINISTRATION

Population:

1913	97,227,000
1921	108,541,000

Key to Map:

States

Territories

BY F. G. COOTES

THE WHITE HOUSE COLLECTION

Woodrow Wilson

BORN:
Staunton, Virginia, December 28, 1856

EDUCATED:
Graduated from Princeton 1879
Graduated from University of Virginia Law School 1882
Graduated from Johns Hopkins (PhD) 1886

MARRIED:
Ellen Axson 1885 (Died 1914)
Edith Bolling Galt 1915

CAREER:
Professor of history, Bryn Mawr 1885-88
Professor of history, Wesleyan 1888-90
Professor of history, Princeton 1890-1902
President of Princeton 1902-10
Governor of New Jersey 1911-13
President 1913-21

DIED:
Washington, D.C., February 3, 1924

29th

WARREN G. HARDING

"We mean to have less of Government in business and more business in Government."

—Address to Congress, 1921

A nation weary of the war years and the lofty idealism of Wilson turned to a good-natured, undistinguished Senator from Ohio in 1920. Harding, the dark-horse Republican candidate, received over seven million votes more than the Democrat James Cox, who ran on Wilson's record. The genial Harding had promised "not heroics, but healing; not nostrums, but normalcy," and the idea of returning to "normalcy" seemed to conform with the mood of the country.

The editor of a small-town newspaper, Harding was an easy-going politician who was everybody's friend. In the eyes of his clever manager Harry Daugherty, Harding had one great asset: he looked like a President. Handsome, with dignified bearing and easy charm, Harding was an impressive figure, and it was as a figurehead, as ceremonial Chief of State, that he best filled the office of President. Neither a leader nor a man of ideas, he seemed to represent the mood and temper of the McKinley administration rather than the two decades of progressive government that had followed; high protective tariffs were established, and both the regulation and taxation of business were reduced. Once again the Government seemed to be at the service of the privileged few.

With the return to "normalcy" came rumors of corruption in high places—at the Cabinet level. Daugherty, who had become Attorney General, was later discovered to have freely sold his influence, and Secretary of the Interior Albert Fall was eventually convicted for accepting $100,000 from private oil interests. But the public—as well as the President himself—knew nothing of these scandals in the summer of 1923 when Harding took a trip to Alaska. Harding learned the details on his return trip, and apparently he never recovered from the shock, for he died rather mysteriously in San Francisco only a few days later. The country mourned the passing of the warm-hearted man who had symbolized the tranquil, pre-war America, perhaps sensing that such "normalcy" was as irrevocably lost as was their President.

THE UNITED STATES DURING HARDING'S ADMINISTRATION

Population:

1921	105,541,000
1923	111,950,000

Key to Map:

States

Territories

BY HENRY R. RITTENBERG THE NEW-YORK HISTORICAL SOCIETY

Born:
Corsica, Ohio, November 2, 1865

Educated:
Attended Ohio Central College 1879–82

Married:
Florence De Wolfe Kling 1891

Career:
Editor of the Marion *Star* 1884–
Member of Ohio Legislature 1900–04
Lieutenant-Governor of Ohio 1904–06
U. S. Senator 1915–21
President 1921–23

Died:
San Francisco, California, August 2, 1923

30th

CALVIN COOLIDGE

"Economy is idealism in its most practical form."

—INAUGURAL ADDRESS, 1925

THE sixth Vice-President to reach the White House through the death of a President, Coolidge differed markedly from the man he succeeded: Harding was easy-going and chatty, Coolidge shy and reserved; Harding an inexperienced executive, Coolidge a proven administrator; Harding a man ruled by few defined principles, Coolidge a Yankee with a passion for economy and efficiency. But both believed in less rather than more government; both favored business. "The business of America is business," said Coolidge, in a statement as long as almost any he made.

Somehow the dour, business-like Coolidge was never associated with the scandals of Harding's administration, and he managed to establish his administration as an honest and efficient one. In every position he held—from mayor of Northampton, Mass., to Vice-President—he demonstrated what he meant by efficient government by working long hours himself. "We need more of the office desk and less of the show window in politics," he said, and he demonstrated this once again by being a hard-working President.

The times were good, business prospered (although farmers suffered), and the industrious New Englander in the White House gained public favor. In 1924 the country showed its approval by electing him for another term. In the years that followed he continued to effect economies in government. In foreign affairs he was less successful, for the Senate blocked U. S. participation in the World Court, and the U. S. was forced to increase expenditures for naval armaments after the failure of the Geneva Conference on arms limitation in 1927.

Whether Coolidge's Yankee cunning led him to realize that all was not as sound as it seemed in the U. S. economy, or whether he had simply had enough, in August 1927, with characteristic brevity, he announced, "I do not choose to run for President in 1928." No one could change his mind. The man who had worked to maintain stability was determined to leave the White House while the country was enjoying stable and prosperous times.

THE UNITED STATES DURING COOLIDGE'S ADMINISTRATION

POPULATION:

1923 111,950,000
1929 121,770,000

KEY TO MAP:

States

Territories

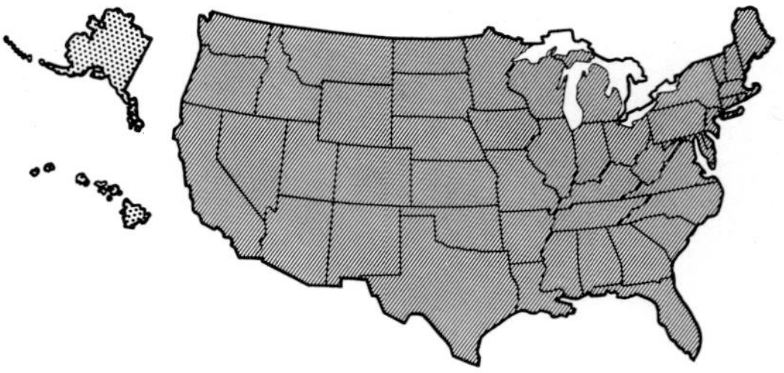

BY WAYMAN ADAMS

THE UNION LEAGUE CLUB, NEW YORK
COURTESY THE FRICK ART REFERENCE LIBRARY

Calvin Coolidge

Born:
Plymouth, Vermont, July 4, 1872

Educated:
Graduated from Amherst College 1895

Married:
Grace Anne Goodhue 1905

Career:
Lawyer 1897–
City Councilman, Northampton, Massachusetts 1899
City Solicitor 1900–01
Clerk of the Courts 1904
Member of Massachusetts Legislature 1907–08; 1912–15
Mayor of Northampton 1910–11
Lieutenant Governor of Massachusetts 1916–18
Governor 1919–20
Vice-President 1921–23
President 1923–29

Died:
Northampton, Massachusetts, January 5, 1933

31st

HERBERT HOOVER

"The greatness of America has grown out of a political and social system and a method of control of economic forces distinctly its own—our American system. . . ."

—RUGGED INDIVIDUALISM, 1928

HERBERT HOOVER was one of those Presidents, like the Adamses and Madison, whose greatest contribution was *not* made in the White House. For Hoover, an extraordinarily successful mining engineer and administrator, the Presidency was a time of trial: he was elected on a "prosperity" platform during the 1928 boom, but the stock market crash and the grinding depression that followed proved to be harsh contradictions to his campaign optimism.

Orphaned at nine, Hoover learned the virtues and rewards of hard work at an early age: he put himself through the first class at Stanford and became a phenomenal success as a mining engineer before he was thirty. Known and respected in international mining circles, he gained world-wide fame when he directed emergency relief activities in Europe during World War I. By the end of the war he held a unique place in the eyes of the world as a dedicated administrator in the service of the cause of humanity. Success continued to be Hoover's lot when he served as Secretary of Commerce in the Harding and Coolidge cabinets, where he re-organized and expanded the Commerce Department.

Running against the popular Governor of New York, Alfred E. Smith, in 1928, Hoover was again successful, gaining more popular votes than any previous candidate. But when Hoover took office, vast forces were at work: the stock market collapsed, the booming industrial complex of the United States broke down, and no individual—not even Hoover with all the powers of the Presidency—could cope with the disaster. He instituted measures to stimulate business with government aid, but the depression continued throughout his years in office. He was overwhelmingly defeated running for re-election in 1932.

THE UNITED STATES DURING HOOVER'S ADMINISTRATION

POPULATION:

1929	121,770,000
1933	125,579,000

KEY TO MAP:

States

Territories

BY G. B. TORREY

THE UNION LEAGUE CLUB, NEW YORK
COURTESY THE FRICK ART REFERENCE LIBRARY

Herbert Hoover

Born:
West Branch, Iowa, August 10, 1874

Educated:
Graduated from Stanford 1895

Married:
Lou Henry 1899

Career:
Mining engineer 1895–1914
Chairman of American Relief Committee, London 1914–15
Commissioner for Belgian Relief 1915–19
U. S. Food Administrator 1917–19
Supreme Economic Council 1919–21
Secretary of Commerce 1921–28
President 1929–33
Chairman, Commission on Organization of Government 1947, 1953

Died:
New York City, October 20, 1964

32nd

FRANKLIN D. ROOSEVELT

"The world order which we seek is the co-operation of free countries, working together in a friendly, civilized society."

—Four Freedoms Address, 1941

Franklin D. Roosevelt, the most controversial President of modern times, was swept into office by an electorate that sought new solutions to the haunting problems of the Depression. In his campaign Roosevelt promised new methods of attack, and once in office, he introduced far-reaching social and economic reforms to stimulate the economy and relieve the distress of millions of unemployed. In thus extending the influence of the Federal Government farther than ever before into the social and economic life of the country, Roosevelt introduced a new concept of government that has continued to be warmly debated, although a number of measures considered radical in 1933 are recognized as necessary today.

Franklin Roosevelt's path to the Presidency strikingly paralleled his fifth cousin Theodore's: born to wealth, he, too, was taught by private tutors, attended Harvard and Columbia, served as New York state legislator, Assistant Secretary of the Navy and Governor of New York; he also ran for Vice-President, but, unlike Theodore, Franklin was defeated. Shortly after this defeat—in 1920—his career almost ended when he was stricken with infantile paralysis, but he recovered sufficiently to return to active life.

The only President to serve more than two terms, Roosevelt was re-elected in 1936, 1940, and 1944. Domestic problems dominated his first term, but by the middle of the second, the U. S. began to recognize the aggressiveness of the Axis powers as a serious threat to world peace. Roosevelt offered U. S. aid to the Allied Powers and, after the attack on Pearl Harbor, he directed the greatest total war effort—military and civilian—in all history. To make America "the arsenal of democracy" the Government took on war powers to control every important phase of industrial production and civilian consumption. Roosevelt met with Churchill and Stalin at Teheran in 1943 to plan strategy, and in 1945 at Yalta to plan for peace.

Roosevelt was in Warm Springs, Georgia, preparing a speech for the San Francisco U. N. Conference when he died suddenly. A few months later the war was over: the man who had broken the two-term precedent and taken on vast powers to lead the country to victory in the world's most terrible war proved to be one of its last casualties.

THE UNITED STATES DURING ROOSEVELT'S ADMINISTRATION

Population:

1933	125,579,000
1945	132,481,000

Key to Map:

States

Territories

BY FRANK O. SALISBURY

THE FRANKLIN D. ROOSEVELT LIBRARY
COURTESY THE NEW YORK GRAPHIC SOCIETY

Franklin D. Roosevelt

Born:
Hyde Park, New York, January 30, 1882

Educated:
Graduated from Harvard 1904
Graduated from Columbia Law School 1907

Married:
Anna Eleanor Roosevelt 1905

Career:
Lawyer 1907–
Member of New York Legislature 1911–13
Assistant Secretary of the Navy 1913–20
Governor of New York 1929–33
President 1933–45

Died:
Warm Springs, Georgia, April 12, 1945

33rd

HARRY S. TRUMAN

"The responsibility of the great states is to serve and not to dominate the world."

—Address to Congress, 1945

In succeeding to the office that Roosevelt held through twelve years of depression, world tension and war, Harry Truman faced the greatest challenge ever to confront a U. S. Vice-President. Thrust without warning into the role of world leader, he was immediately burdened with two almost overwhelming tasks: leading the U. S. to final victory and planning a sound world peace. Truman emerged from the shadow of his predecessor, dealt courageously with these problems, and in 1948 established himself as President in his own right when he upset all predictions by defeating Governor Thomas E. Dewey of New York.

As a young man Truman had done farming, served in World War I as an artillery Captain and been partner in a haberdashery; in 1922 he entered politics. After studying law and serving as county judge, he was elected U. S. Senator in 1934. During World War II the Truman Committee became known for its careful investigation of defense spending; Harry Truman won national prominence and, in 1944, the Vice-Presidential nomination.

Truman's administration was filled with momentous events: in the first year he met with Churchill and Stalin at Potsdam; he made the historic decision to use the atomic bomb; Germany and Japan surrendered; and the U. S. accepted the United Nations' Charter. In the following years came the Marshall Plan—with aid for Europe; Point Four—with aid and technical assistance for under-developed countries; NATO; and in 1950 the Korean War—the most dramatic step the U. S. took to contain Communism. Sending troops to Korea to fight a "limited" war and deciding to use the atomic bomb represented totally new kinds of decisions for a President; in making them, the man who said "The buck stops here" brought the country face to face with the two greatest problems of the day: nuclear power and the threat of Communism.

THE UNITED STATES DURING TRUMAN'S ADMINISTRATION

Population:

1945 132,481,000
1953 158,434,000

Key to Map:

States

Territories

BY M. G. KEMPTON

THE WHITE HOUSE COLLECTION

Born:
Lamar, Missouri, May 8, 1884

Educated:
Kansas City Law School 1923–25

Married:
Elizabeth Wallace 1919

Career:
Reporter, timekeeper, bank clerk in Kansas City 1901–06
Farmer 1906–17
Army Officer in World War I 1917–19
Owner of haberdashery in Kansas City 1919–22
Judge, Jackson County Court 1922–24
Presiding County Judge 1926–34
U. S. Senator 1935–45
Vice President January 20–April 12, 1945
President 1945–53

Died:
Kansas City, Missouri, December 26, 1972

34th

DWIGHT D. EISENHOWER

"The quest for peace is the statesman's most exacting duty. . . . Practical progress to lasting peace is his fondest hope."

—Geneva Conference Address, 1955

General Dwight D. Eisenhower, the popular hero of World War II, was drafted by the Republican Party to run for President in 1952. In that year the genial "Ike," whose sincerity and good will captured the country, took his place with other U. S. military heroes who have been elevated to the Presidency. Like Zachary Taylor and Ulysses Grant, Eisenhower was a professional soldier who had never held a political office.

In the Army Eisenhower distinguished himself in planning and staff work; during the 1930's he served as special assistant to General Douglas MacArthur, Chief of Staff, and assisted him when he became military adviser to the Philippines. In World War II Eisenhower commanded the North African invasion and later became famous as the man who welded the armies of the allied nations into the mighty force that won the war in Europe.

Elected on a platform of peace, Eisenhower used the powers of the Presidency to reduce world tension: his first year in office he brought the Korean War to an end, and after both the U. S. and Russia developed H-bombs, he proposed an "open-skies" plan for disarmament, as well as plans for an international atom pool for peaceful use. Despite such efforts, the problem of containing Communism continued to be a major concern throughout his administration: the Communists took North Vietnam in 1954, and in 1956 Russian troops reconquered a fighting Hungary that had struggled heroically to win its brief moment of freedom.

The enormous popularity that carried Eisenhower into the White House remained undiminished in 1956, when he again defeated Adlai Stevenson of Illinois. During Eisenhower's second term, racial segregation became a consuming domestic issue, one that reached a climax in September 1957, when the President sent U. S. troops to Little Rock, Arkansas, to maintain order. With the Communist threat continuing to dominate the world scene, Eisenhower made a dramatic world tour for peace. In 1961, when he retired to his Gettysburg farm, the U. S. had reached a state of unparalleled prosperity, but a belligerent and powerful Russia continued to threaten the security of the U. S. and the free world.

THE UNITED STATES DURING EISENHOWER'S ADMINISTRATION

Population:

1953	158,434,000
1961	183,650,000

Key to Map:

Existing States, 1953

New States, 1953-61

BY THOMAS E. STEPHENS THE WHITE HOUSE COLLECTION

Dwight D. Eisenhower

Born:
Denison, Texas, October 14, 1890

Educated:
Graduated from West Point 1915

Married:
Mamie Geneva Doud 1916

Career:
Officer in U. S. Army 1916–
Lieutenant General, Commander-in-Chief of Allied Expeditionary Forces in North Africa 1942
Commanding General of Allied Powers in Europe 1943–45
Chief of Staff, U. S. Army 1945–48
President of Columbia University 1948–50
Supreme Commander of Allied Powers in Europe 1950–52
President 1953–61

Died:
Washington, D.C., March 28, 1969

35th

JOHN F. KENNEDY

"In the long history of the world, only a few generations have been granted the role of defending freedom in its hour of maximum danger. . . . The energy, the faith, the devotion which we bring to this endeavor will light our country and all who serve it, and the glow from that fire can truly light the world."

—Inaugural Address, 1961

The youngest man ever elected President—and the youngest to die in office—John F. Kennedy defeated Vice-President Richard Nixon in the first Presidential election which featured candidates in formal television debates before millions of voters across the nation. A Pulitzer Prize-winning biographer and a Naval hero of World War II, he was the first Catholic to be elected President.

Kennedy was born into a family with a political history: both his grandfathers were active in politics, and his father served as U.S. Ambassador to Great Britain. But Kennedy first won acclaim as an author when his Harvard honors thesis, published as *Why England Slept,* became a best seller. In the war he was decorated for saving his PT-boat crew when a Japanese destroyer cut his boat in two. In 1946 he entered politics and was elected to Congress; six years later he became a Senator.

Publication of Kennedy's prize-winning book *Profiles in Courage* coincided with his emergence on the national political scene. In 1956 he narrowly missed the Democratic nomination for Vice-President; by 1960 he was a leading contender for the Presidency. He defeated Nixon in one of the closest of Presidential elections.

On taking office, Kennedy delivered a stirring Inaugural Address: he appealed to all peoples for restraint and co-operation in building a safe—and a free—world in the age of nuclear weapons. In his first year he introduced new programs—the Alliance for Progress and the Peace Corps, weathered the Bay-of-Pigs disaster, and met Communist challenges throughout the world. His space program bore fruit in 1962 when Astronaut John Glenn, Jr. orbited the earth; but he also faced three crises: with Big Steel over prices, with Mississippi over integration, and with Russia over missile sites in Cuba. By challenging the Communist build-up in Cuba, Kennedy effected the first significant Russian retreat of the Cold War. In 1963 he reached an agreement with Russia to limit nuclear tests and offered controversial civil-rights and tax bills to Congress. Before Congress acted, on November 22, while President Kennedy was in Dallas, Texas, on a speaking tour with his wife, he was assassinated by a sniper—a tragedy that shocked the world.

THE UNITED STATES DURING KENNEDY'S ADMINISTRATION

Population:

1961	183,650,000
1963	190,417,000

Key to Map:

States

BY ALFRED EISENSTAEDT

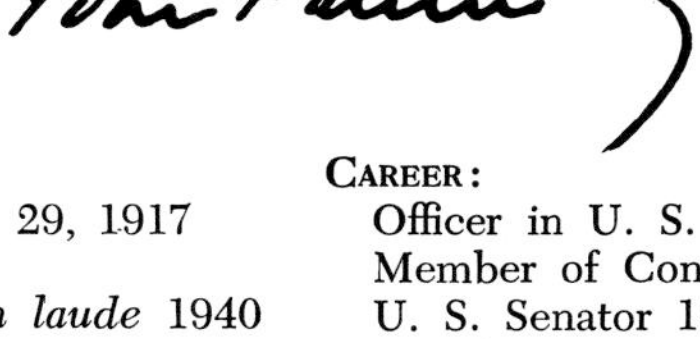

Born:
Brookline, Massachusetts, May 29, 1917

Educated:
Graduated from Harvard *cum laude* 1940

Married:
Jacqueline Lee Bouvier 1953

Career:
Officer in U. S. Navy 1942–45
Member of Congress 1947–53
U. S. Senator 1953–61
President 1961–63

Died:
Dallas, Texas, November 22, 1963

36th

LYNDON B. JOHNSON

"If we fail now, then we will have forgotten in abundance what we learned in hardship: that democracy rests on faith; freedom asks more than it gives; and the judgment of God is harshest on those who are most favored."

—INAUGURAL ADDRESS, 1965

LYNDON B. JOHNSON is the eighth Vice-President to take the place of a President who died in office, the fourth to be elected to a new term. One of the most experienced national political figures ever elected Vice-President, he was sworn into office at Dallas, Texas, shortly after President Kennedy was assassinated.

Like his predecessor, Johnson was born into a family with a political heritage: his father and grandfather were both in politics; when Lyndon was born, his grandfather predicted he would be a U.S. Senator.

By the time he was forty Johnson had achieved what his grandfather had predicted. In the Senate his abilities to lead and persuade made themselves felt; as Senate Majority Leader during President Eisenhower's administrations, Johnson established himself as a skillful and commanding political leader. He provided the Republican President bipartisan support for such critical legislation as the civil-rights bill that was passed in 1957, the first civil-rights legislation in over eighty years.

In 1960 Johnson surprised many political friends when he ran as Vice-President on the Kennedy ticket. After becoming President, he moved firmly to stabilize the Government and to support Kennedy programs at home and abroad.

In November 1964, Johnson defeated Senator Goldwater, winning over 61 per cent of the popular vote. In 1965 he sent Congress his programs to build "The Great Society." One of the most productive in Congressional history, that session turned into law bills on medicare, school and college aid, voting rights, and anti-poverty measures. During 1965 Johnson also increased the U.S. commitment in Vietnam and, in December, directed the first American air raid against North Vietnam. The bombing and the continued increases of U.S. troops in Vietnam led to large, occasionally violent demonstrations. The country was also torn by riots in predominantly Negro sections of major cities.

On March 31, 1968, President Johnson stunned the Nation by announcing he would not run for re-election. In October he announced a bombing halt that led to more serious peace talks in Paris. The closing days of his Administration saw a flawless Apollo flight to the moon and indications from the Paris talks of improved prospects for peace in Vietnam.

THE UNITED STATES DURING JOHNSON'S ADMINISTRATION

POPULATION

1963	190,417,000
1969	202,314,064

KEY TO MAP:
States

BY YOUSUF KARSH THE WHITE HOUSE COLLECTION

Lyndon B. Johnson

BORN:
Stonewall, Texas, August 27, 1908

EDUCATED:
Graduated from Southwest Texas State Teachers College 1930

MARRIED:
Claudia (Lady Bird) Taylor 1934

CAREER:
School teacher in Texas 1930-31
Congressional secretary 1931-37
Member of Congress 1937-49
Officer in U.S. Navy 1941-42
U.S. Senator 1949-61
Vice-President January 20, 1961-November 22, 1963
President 1963-69

DIED:
San Antonio, Texas, January 22, 1973

37th

RICHARD M. NIXON

"The peace we seek to win is not victory over any other people, but the peace that comes "with healing in its wings;" with compassion for those who have suffered; with understanding for those who have opposed us; with the opportunity for all the peoples of this Earth to choose their own destiny."

—INAUGURAL ADDRESS, 1969

The first President to resign from office, Richard Nixon removed himself from the Presidency August 9, 1974, after investigations of the Watergate cover-up finally revealed that he had acted illegally and that it was clear that he could not survive the impeachment proceedings then in progress. One month later he was granted an unqualified pardon by his successor.

Nixon first won national attention in 1948 when, as a member of the House Un-American Activities Committee, he forced the confrontation that led to the perjury conviction of Alger Hiss. As Vice-President in 1959, he conducted the famous "kitchen debate" with Khrushchev in Moscow.

After a seven-year absence, Nixon returned to national office in 1968 when he defeated Vice-President Hubert Humphrey to become the 37th President. During his first term, an American became the first man to walk on the moon, opposition to U.S. participation in Vietnam took the form of mass demonstrations in U.S. cities, and the U.S. and the Soviet Union began strategic arms limitations talks.

Most significant were Nixon's efforts to resolve international problems and promote world peace. In February 1972 he became the first U.S. President ever to visit China. His talks with Premier Chou En-lai and Chairman Mao Tse-tung led to an historic agreement pledging peaceful co-existence. In May 1972 Nixon and Chairman Brezhnev of the Soviet Union signed a treaty which reduced anti-ballistic missile deployment and limited the number of offensive strategic weapons—the first significant action to limit the nuclear arms race.

On June 17, 1972, four men were arrested for breaking into the Democratic National Headquarters in the Watergate. Nixon and his aides denied involvement, and they succeeded in a cover-up of their involvement in this and other illegal actions, so that these were not significant issues in the 1972 election, which Nixon easily won.

Nixon began 1973 by withdrawing all U.S. troops from Vietnam. During the next eighteen months, the Senate Watergate hearings, the revelation of the White House tapes, the trials of over twenty Nixon aides, and, finally, the Supreme Court's 8-0 decision forcing Nixon to surrender crucial tapes to the Special Prosecutor, brought out the facts that assured Nixon's impeachment if he did not resign.

THE UNITED STATES DURING NIXON'S ADMINISTRATION

POPULATION:
1969 202,314,064
1974 211,210,000

KEY TO MAP:
States

BY PHILIPPE HALSMAN — THE WHITE HOUSE COLLECTION

Richard Nixon

BORN:
Yorba Linda, California, January 9, 1913

EDUCATED:
Graduated from Whittier College 1934
Graduated from Duke University Law School 1937

MARRIED:
Thelma Catherine Patricia Ryan 1940

CAREER:
Lawyer 1937-41, 1961-69
Attorney, U.S. Office of Emergency Management 1942
Officer in U.S. Navy 1942-46
Member of Congress 1947-51
U.S. Senator 1951-53
Vice-President 1953-61
President 1969–August 9, 1974

38th

GERALD R. FORD

"My fellow Americans, our long national nightmare is over. Our Constitution works. Our great republic is a government of laws and not of men.Here, the people rule. . . ."

—INAUGURAL ADDRESS, 1974

America's first unelected President, Gerald Ford assumed the office of President August 9, 1974, when President Nixon resigned. Eight months before, Ford had become the first appointed Vice-President. He was the first to assume both positions under the provisions of the Twenty-Fifth Amendment.

An exceptional football player at the University of Michigan, Ford coached football at Yale while studying law there. In World War II he served as a naval officer in the Pacific.

In 1948 Ford won a seat in Congress and soon gained a reputation for his ability to deal with the complexities of defense budgets. Through the 1950s and 1960s he built a record that was moderate to conservative. During those years he declined to run for governor of Michigan or U.S. senator; instead he remained in the House and, in 1960, won the position of GOP Conference Chairman. Two years later he was elected Minority Leader.

Ford began his Presidency with immense popular support. His sudden pardon of Nixon brought sharp criticism, but, as time passed, his sincerity and candor helped restore faith in the Presidency. On taking office, he stated he would not be a candidate in 1976, but in July 1975 he announced he would run. That year he signed the Helsinki accords with the USSR and thirty other nations, and met with Chinese leaders in Peking, seeking to maintain stable, if limited, relations.

By early 1976 it was clear that Ford had succeeded in bringing the country out of the recession, and his "peace and prosperity" campaign brought victories over Ronald Reagan in early primaries. But, although he presided over a glorious Bincentennial Fourth of July and the economic recovery continued, he narrowly defeated Reagan (1187 to 1071).

Although the nation's economic recovery slowed during the campaign and Democratic candidate Carter dominated the first Presidential television debates since 1960, Ford came from behind to make a close race of the election (297 to 241 electoral votes). Ford was the first incumbent since Herbert Hoover to lose a Presidential election.

THE UNITED STATES DURING FORD'S ADMINISTRATION

POPULATION:
1974 211,210,000
1977 216,532,667

KEY TO MAP:
States

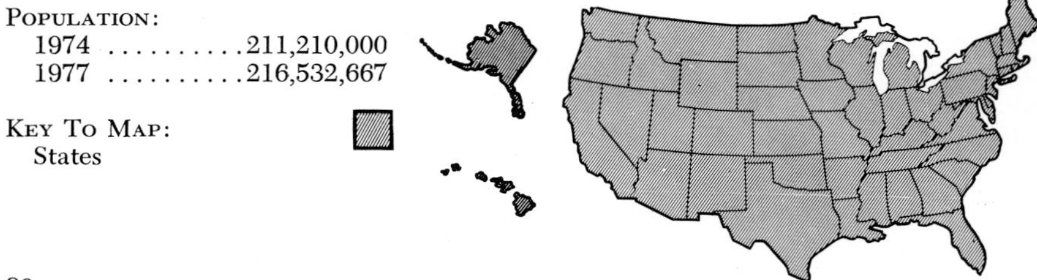

DAVID KENNERLY

Gerald R. Ford

BORN:
Omaha, Nebraska, July 14, 1913

EDUCATED:
Graduated from University of Michigan 1935
Graduated from Yale Law School 1941

MARRIED:
Elizabeth Boomer Warren 1948

CAREER:
Asst. football coach, Yale University 1935–41
Lawyer 1941–
Officer in U.S. Navy 1942–45
Member of Congress 1949–73
House Minority Leader 1965–73
Vice-President December 6, 1973–August 9, 1974
President August 9, 1974–January 20, 1977

JAMES E. CARTER

"Two centuries ago our nation's birth was a milestone in the long quest for freedom, but the bold and brilliant dream which excited the founders of our nation still awaits its consummation. I have no new dream to set forth today, but rather urge a fresh faith in the old dream."

INAUGURAL ADDRESS, 1977

In the first Presidential election supported, in part, by Federal funds, and the second involving nationally televised debates, Jimmy Carter came from comparative obscurity to capture the Democratic nomination and the Presidency, the first man from the Deep South elected President since the Civil War.

As a young naval officer, Carter served in the nuclear submarine program under Admiral Hyman Rickover. After his father died, Carter resigned from the Navy and returned to Georgia to operate the family farm. His father had served in the Georgia senate, and Carter's first public service was on the local school board. In 1962, as a little-known candidate, he defeated an experienced state senator, winning a disputed election in which his opponent used illegal tactics. In 1966 Carter ran for the Democratic nomination for governor, but lost to Lester Maddox; in 1970 he was elected.

Carter's Presidency was marked by a continuing commitment to human rights, a quest for Arab-Israeli peace, and, at the end, an interminable hostage crisis. In 1977 Carter proposed a comprehensive Energy Program—calling the problem "the moral equivalent of war," created a new Energy Department, and signed the controversial Panama Canal treaties. In 1978 Carter helped bring Egypt's Anwar Sadat and Israel's Menachen Begin to agree on the historic Camp David Accords, establishing a "framework for peace" in the Middle East. In 1979 the U.S. established diplomatic relations with Communist China and ended relations with Nationalist China on Taiwan; and Carter and Brezhnev signed the SALT II Treaty, but the U.S. Senate withheld ratification. That year world oil prices more than doubled and inflation in the U.S. soared.

Iranian seizure of Americans in the U.S. embassy in Tehran in November 1979 created a crisis that dominated the nation's concerns until they were released Carter's last day. To protest the Soviet's invasion of Afghanistan, Carter instituted a grain and trade embargo and advocated a boycott of the 1980 Olympics in Moscow.

Carter fought off the challenge of Senator Edward Kennedy for his Party's nomination, but in the election he was roundly defeated by Republican Ronald Reagan (489 to 49 electoral votes).

THE UNITED STATES DURING CARTER'S ADMINISTRATION

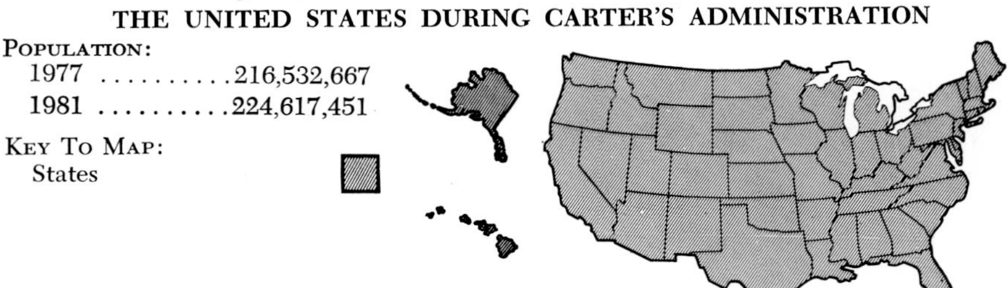

POPULATION:
1977 216,532,667
1981 224,617,451

KEY TO MAP:
States

THE WHITE HOUSE

Jimmy Carter

BORN:
Plains, Georgia, October 1, 1924

EDUCATED:
Graduated from U.S. Naval Academy 1946

MARRIED:
Rosalynn Smith 1946

CAREER:
Officer in the U.S. Navy 1946-54
Farmer 1954-
State Senator 1963-66
Governor of Georgia 1971-75
President 1977–81

40th

RONALD W. REAGAN

"With all the creative energy at our command, let us begin an era of national renewal. Let us renew our determination, our courage and our strength. . . . We have every right to dream heroic dreams."
INAUGURAL ADDRESS, 1981

Winning by the greatest electoral margin (525-13) since Franklin Roosevelt defeated Alfred Landon in 1936 (523-8), Ronald Reagan swept 49 States and defeated Democratic candidate Walter Mondale to gain a convincing mandate for the continuation of his conservative programs in a second term. Republicans retained the Senate majority won in 1980.

A comparative latecomer to politics, Reagan achieved national recognition as a leading man in 50 Hollywood movies and as a host for national television programs. He served six terms as president of the Screen Actors' Guild and two terms as president of the Motion Picture Industry Council. Reagan emerged suddenly on the political scene in 1964 when he delivered a speech on television supporting presidential candidate Barry Goldwater. Two years later he was elected governor of California. In two terms he practiced the fiscal responsibility he had preached and won national attention as a political leader.

Reagan's victory over incumbent Jimmy Carter in 1980 represented a profound political shift toward conservatism in the U.S. One of Reagan's first actions was to abolish price controls on domestic oil and gas, creating a free market in those commodities. In Washington, on March 30, 1981, President Reagan was shot and wounded in an assassination attempt. After successful surgery he was able to continue to function as President. That year he won Congressional approval of a tax cut and appointed the first woman — Sandra O'Connor — to the Supreme Court. After a recession in 1982, the U.S. economy began a recovery that endured through the 1984 election. In 1983, the bombing of the U.S. Embassy and the Marine Headquarters in Beirut, the U.S. invasion of Grenada to remove a Marxist regime that had seized power, and U.S. aid to Central American regimes all sparked controversy. In the face of sometimes clamorous opposition, Reagan continued to stress the need for a strong defense, insisting that defense and some benefit programs be spared the budget cuts dictated by the growing budget deficit.

The beginning of Reagan's second term was marked by the opening of new negotiations with the Soviet Union on arms control and a Government-wide effort to plan for continued reductions in the budget deficit — two of the most critical issues of our time.

THE UNITED STATES DURING REAGAN'S ADMINISTRATION

POPULATION:
1981 224,617,451

KEY TO MAP:
States

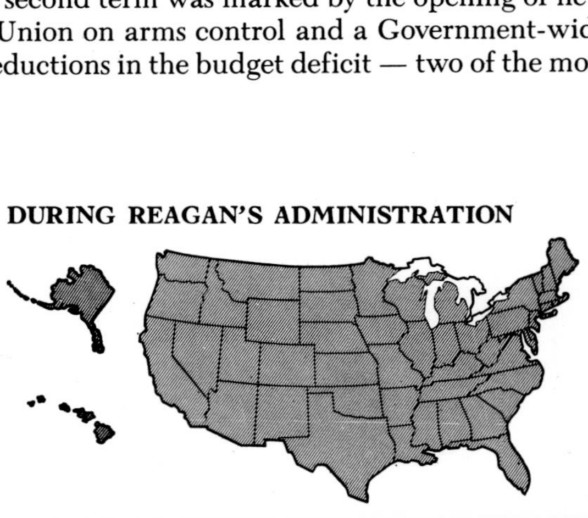

THE WHITE HOUSE

Ronald Reagan

Born:
Tampico, Illinois, February 6, 1911

Educated:
Graduated from Eureka College 1932

Married:
Jane Wyman 1940 (Divorced 1948)
Nancy Davis 1952

Career:
Radio Sportscaster 1932–36
Movie actor 1937–57
Officer in U.S. Army Air Force 1942–45
Television host 1957–65
Governor of California 1966–74
Radio commentator, columnist 1974–
President January 20, 1981–

BIOGRAPHICAL FACTS

President	*Birth Place*	*Date*	*Education*	*Profession*
George Washington	Westmoreland Cy., Va.	1732	Common Schools	Planter
John Adams	Quincy, Mass.	1735	Harvard	Lawyer
Thomas Jefferson	Shadwell, Va.	1743	William & Mary	Lawyer
James Madison	Port Conway, Va.	1751	Princeton	Lawyer
James Monroe	Westmoreland Cy., Va.	1758	William & Mary	Lawyer
John Quincy Adams	Quincy, Mass.	1767	Harvard	Lawyer
Andrew Jackson	Lancaster County, N.C.	1767	Self-Educated	Lawyer
Martin Van Buren	Kinderhook, N. Y.	1782	Common Schools	Lawyer
William H. Harrison	Berkeley, Va.	1773	Hampden-Sydney	Soldier
John Tyler	Greenway, Va.	1790	William & Mary	Lawyer
James K. Polk	Mecklenburg County, N. C.	1795	Univ. of North Carolina	Lawyer
Zachary Taylor	Orange County, Va.	1784	Self-Educated	Soldier
Millard Fillmore	Cayuga County, N. Y.	1800	Self-Educated	Lawyer
Franklin Pierce	Hillsboro, N. H.	1804	Bowdoin	Lawyer
James Buchanan	Franklin County, Pa.	1791	Dickinson College	Lawyer
Abraham Lincoln	Hardin County, Ky.	1809	Self-Educated	Lawyer
Andrew Johnson	Raleigh, N. C.	1808	Self-Educated	Tailor
Ulysses S. Grant	Point Pleasant, Ohio	1822	West Point	Soldier
Rutherford Hayes	Delaware, Ohio	1822	Kenyon, Harvard	Lawyer
James Garfield	Orange, Ohio	1831	Williams	Teacher
Chester Arthur	Fairfield, Vt.	1830	Union College	Lawyer
Grover Cleveland	Caldwell, N. J.	1837	Common Schools	Lawyer
Benjamin Harrison	North Bend, Ohio	1833	Miami University	Lawyer
William McKinley	Niles, Ohio	1843	Allegheny College	Lawyer
Theodore Roosevelt	New York, N. Y.	1858	Harvard, Columbia	Lawyer
William H. Taft	Cincinnati, Ohio	1857	Yale	Lawyer
Woodrow Wilson	Staunton, Va.	1856	Princeton, Johns Hopkins	Teacher
Warren G. Harding	Corsica, Ohio	1865	Ohio Central College	Journalist
Calvin Coolidge	Plymouth, Vt.	1872	Amherst	Lawyer
Herbert Hoover	West Branch, Iowa	1874	Stanford	Engineer
Franklin D. Roosevelt	Hyde Park, N. Y.	1882	Harvard, Columbia	Lawyer
Harry S. Truman	Lamar, Mo.	1884	Kansas City Law	Lawyer
Dwight D. Eisenhower	Denison, Texas	1890	West Point	Soldier
John F. Kennedy	Brookline, Mass.	1917	Harvard	Author
Lyndon B. Johnson	Stonewall, Texas	1908	Southwest Texas State Teachers College	Public Official
Richard M. Nixon	Yorba Linda, California	1913	Whittier, Duke	Lawyer
Gerald R. Ford	Omaha, Nebraska	1913	Univ. of Michigan, Yale	Lawyer
James E. Carter	Plains, Georgia	1924	U. S. Naval Academy	Farmer
Ronald W. Reagan	Tampico, Illinois	1911	Eureka College	Actor

Term	*Place of Death*	*Date*	*Place of Burial*
April 30, 1789–March 4, 1797	Mount Vernon, Va.	1799	Mount Vernon, Va.
March 4, 1797–March 4, 1801	Quincy, Mass.	1826	Quincy, Mass.
March 4, 1801–March 4, 1809	Monticello, Va.	1826	Monticello, Va.
March 4, 1809–March 4, 1817	Montpelier, Va.	1836	Montpelier, Va.
March 4, 1817–March 4, 1825	New York, N. Y.	1831	Richmond, Va.
March 4, 1825–March 4, 1829	Washington, D. C.	1848	Quincy, Mass.
March 4, 1829–March 4, 1837	Hermitage, Tenn.	1845	Hermitage, Tenn.
March 4, 1837–March 4, 1841	Kinderhook, N. Y.	1862	Kinderhook, N. Y.
March 4, 1841–April 4, 1841	Washington. D. C.	1841	North Bend, Ohio
April 4, 1841–March 4, 1845	Richmond, Va.	1862	Richmond, Va.
March 4, 1845–March 4, 1849	Nashville, Tenn.	1849	Nashville, Tenn.
March 4, 1849–July 9, 1850	Washington, D. C.	1850	Louisville, Ky.
July 9, 1850–March 4, 1853	Buffalo, N. Y.	1874	Buffalo, N. Y.
March 4, 1853–March 4, 1857	Concord, N. H.	1869	Concord, N. H.
March 4, 1857–March 4, 1861	Lancaster, Pa.	1868	Lancaster, Pa.
March 4, 1861–April 15, 1865	Washington, D. C.	1865	Springfield, Ill.
April 15, 1865–March 4, 1869	Carter's Station, Tenn.	1875	Greenville, Tenn.
March 4, 1869–March 4, 1877	Mt. McGregor, N. Y.	1885	New York, N. Y.
March 4, 1877–March 4, 1881	Fremont, Ohio	1893	Fremont, Ohio
March 4, 1881–September 19, 1881	Elberon, N. J.	1881	Cleveland, Ohio
September 19, 1881–March 4, 1885	New York, N. Y.	1886	Albany, N. Y.
March 4, 1885–March 4, 1889	Princeton, N. J.	1908	Princeton, N. J.
March 4, 1893–March 4, 1897			
March 4, 1889–March 4, 1893	Indianapolis, Ind.	1901	Indianapolis, Ind.
March 4, 1897–September 14, 1901	Buffalo, N. Y.	1901	Canton, Ohio
September 14, 1901–March 4, 1909	Oyster Bay, N. Y.	1919	Oyster Bay, N. Y.
March 4, 1909–March 4, 1913	Washington, D. C.	1930	Arlington Cemetery
March 4, 1913–March 4, 1921	Washington, D. C.	1924	Washington, D. C.
March 4, 1921–August 2, 1923	San Francisco, Cal.	1923	Marion, Ohio
August 3, 1923–March 4, 1929	Northampton, Mass.	1933	Plymouth, Vt.
March 4, 1929–March 4, 1933	New York, N. Y.	1964	West Branch, Iowa
March 4, 1933–April 12, 1945	Warm Springs, Ga.	1945	Hyde Park, N. Y.
April 12, 1945–January 20, 1953	Kansas City, Mo.	1972	Independence, Mo.
January 20, 1953–January 20, 1961	Washington, D.C.	1969	Abilene, Kan.
January 20, 1961–November 22, 1963	Dallas, Texas	1963	Arlington Cemetery
November 22, 1963–January 20, 1969	San Antonio, Texas	1973	Johnson City, Texas
January 20, 1969–August 9, 1974			
August 9, 1974–January 20, 1977			
January 20, 1977–January 20, 1981			
January 20, 1981			

PRESIDENTIAL ELECTIONS

Date	*President*	*Vice-Presidents*	*Party*	*Popular Vote*	*Electoral Vote*
1789	George Washington	John Adams	No Party	Unknown	69
1792	George Washington	John Adams	Federalist	Unknown	132
1796	John Adams	Thomas Jefferson	Federalist	Unknown	71
1800	Thomas Jefferson	Aaron Burr	Dem.-Rep	Unknown	73
1804	Thomas Jefferson	George Clinton	Dem.-Rep.	Unknown	162
1808	James Madison	George Clinton	Dem.-Rep.	Unknown	122
1812	James Madison	Elbridge Gerry	Dem.-Rep.	Unknown	128
1816	James Monroe	Daniel Tompkins	Dem.-Rep.	Unknown	183
1820	James Monroe	Daniel Tompkins	Dem.-Rep.	Unknown	231
1824	John Quincy Adams	John Calhoun	Nat. Rep.	105,321	84
1828	Andrew Jackson	John Calhôun	Democrat	647,276	178
1832	Andrew Jackson	Martin Van Buren	Democrat	687,502	219
1836	Martin Van Buren	Richard Johnson	Democrat	762,678	170
1840	William H. Harrison	John Tyler	Whig	1,275,017	234
1844	James K. Polk	George Dallas	Democrat	1,337,243	170
1848	Zachary Taylor	Millard Fillmore	Whig	1,360,099	163
1852	Franklin Pierce	William King	Democrat	1,601,274	254
1856	James Buchanan	John Breckinridge	Democrat	1,838,169	174
1860	Abraham Lincoln	Hannibal Hamlin	Republican	1,866,452	180
1864	Abraham Lincoln	Andrew Johnson	Republican	2,213,665	212
1868	Ulysses S. Grant	Schuyler Colfax	Republican	3,012,833	214
1872	Ulysses S. Grant	Henry Wilson	Republican	3,597,132	286
1876	Rutherford B. Hayes	William Wheeler	Republican	4,036,298	185
1880	James A. Garfield	Chester Arthur	Republican	4,454,416	214
1884	Grover Cleveland	Thomas Hendricks	Democrat	4,874,986	219
1888	Benjamin Harrison	Levi Morton	Republican	5,444,337	233
1892	Grover Cleveland	Adlai Stevenson	Democrat	5,556,918	277
1896	William McKinley	Garret Hobart	Republican	7,104,779	271
1900	William McKinley	Theodore Roosevel	Republican	7,207,923	292
1904	Theodore Roosevelt	Charles Fairbanks	Republican	7,623,486	336
1908	William H. Taft	James Sherman	Republican	7,678,908	321
1912	Woodrow Wilson	Thomas Marshall	Democrat	6,293,454	435
1916	Woodrow Wilson	Thomas Marshall	Democrat	9,129,606	277
1920	Warren G. Harding	Calvin Coolidge	Republican	16,152,200	404
1924	Calvin Coolidge	Charles Dawes	Republican	15,725,016	382
1928	Herbert Hoover	Charles Curtis	Republican	21,391,381	444
1932	Franklin D. Roosevelt	John Garner	Democrat	22,821,857	472
1936	Franklin D. Roosevelt	John Garner	Democrat	27,751,597	523
1940	Franklin D. Roosevelt	Henry Wallace	Democrat	27,244,160	449
1944	Franklin D. Roosevelt	Harry Truman	Democrat	25,602,504	432
1948	Harry S. Truman	Alben Barkley	Democrat	24,105,695	303
1952	Dwight D. Eisenhower	Richard Nixon	Republican	33,778,963	442
1956	Dwight D. Eisenhower	Richard Nixon	Republican	35,581,003	457
1960	John F. Kennedy	Lyndon Johnson	Democrat	34,226,925	300
1964	Lyndon B. Johnson	Hubert Humphrey	Democrat	42,676,220	486
1968	Richard M. Nixon	Spiro T. Agnew	Republican	31,770,237	301
1972	Richard M. Nixon	Spiro T. Agnew	Republican	45,767,218	521
1976	James E. Carter	Walter F. Mondale	Democrat	40,291,626	297
1980	Ronald W. Reagan	George Bush	Republican	42,797,153	489
1984	Ronald Reagan	George Bush	Republican	52,609,797	525

Defeated Candidate	*Party*	*Popular Vote*	*Electoral Vote*
No Opponent			
No Opponent			
Thomas Jefferson	Democrat-Republican	Unknown	68
Aaron Burr	Democrat-Republican	Unknown	73
Charles Pinckney	Federalist	Unknown	14
Charles Pinckney	Federalist	Unknown	47
DeWitt Clinton	Federalist	Unknown	89
Rufus King	Federalist	Unknown	34
John Quincy Adams	Democrat-Republican	Unknown	1
Andrew Jackson	Democrat	155,872	99
Henry Clay	Democrat-Republican	46,587	37
William Crawford	Democrat-Republican	44,282	41
John Quincy Adams	National Republican	508,064	83
Henry Clay	Democrat-Republican	530,189	49
William H. Harrison	Whig	548,007	73
Martin Van Buren	Democrat	1,129,102	60
Henry Clay	Whig	1,299,062	105
Lewis Cass	Democrat	1,220,544	127
Winfield Scott	Whig	1,386,580	42
John C. Fremont	Republican	1,341,264	114
Stephen A. Douglas	Democrat	1,375,157	12
John C. Breckinridge	Democrat	845,763	72
George B. McClellan	Democrat	1,805,237	21
Horatio Seymour	Democrat	2,703,249	80
Horace Greeley	Democrat	2,834,079	66
Samuel J. Tilden	Democrat	4,300,590	184
Winfield S. Hancock	Democrat	4,444,952	155
James G. Blaine	Republican	4,851,981	182
Grover Cleveland	Democrat	5,540,309	168
Benjamin Harrison	Republican	5,176,108	145
James Weaver	People's	1,041,028	22
William J. Bryan	Democrat	6,502,925	176
William J. Bryan	Democrat	6,358,138	155
Alton B. Parker	Democrat	5,077,911	140
William J. Bryan	Democrat	6,409,104	162
Theodore Roosevelt	Progressive	4,119,538	88
William H. Taft	Republican	3,484,980	8
Charles E. Hughes	Republican	8,538,221	254
James M. Cox	Democrat	9,147,353	127
John W. Davis	Democrat	8,386,503	136
Robert M. LaFollette	Progressive	4,822,856	13
Alfred E. Smith	Democrat	15,016,443	87
Herbert Hoover	Republican	15,761,841	59
Alfred Landon	Republican	16,679,583	8
Wendell L. Willkie	Republican	22,305,198	82
Thomas E. Dewey	Republican	22,006,278	99
Thomas E. Dewey	Republican	21,969,170	189
J. Strom Thurmond	States Rights	1,169,021	39
Henry A. Wallace	Progressive	1,156,103	0
Adlai E. Stevenson	Democrat	27,314,992	89
Adlai E. Stevenson	Democrat	25,738,765	73
Richard M. Nixon	Republican	34,108,662	223
Barry M. Goldwater	Republican	26,860,314	52
Hubert Humphrey	Democrat	31,270,533	191
George Wallace	American	9,897,141	46
George McGovern	Democrat	28,357,668	17
Gerald Ford	Republican	38,563,089	241
James Carter	Democrat	34,434,100	49
Walter Mondale	Democrat	36,450,613	13

ACKNOWLEDGEMENTS

The author gratefully acknowledges his indebtedness to the individuals and organizations who made it possible for the present collection of portraits to be assembled:

The Century Association, New York

Mrs. Ralph E. Phillips and Mrs. A. Robert Forbes, The Corcoran Gallery of Art

The Franklin D. Roosevelt Library

Miss Mildred Steinbach, The Frick Art Reference Library

Mrs. Jewel S. Baker, the National Collection of Fine Arts

Mr. Huntington Cairns, Mr. William Campbell, Mrs. Betty S. Gajdusek, and Mrs. Mildred Kirsher, The National Gallery of Art

The New York Graphic Society

The New-York Historical Society

Congressman James Roosevelt

The Union League Club, New York

Mr. Pierre Salinger, Miss Barbara Coleman, The White House

Signatures of the Presidents are from the Library of Congress, and from *Presidents on Parade* by Hirst Milhollen and Milton Kaplan, courtesy of the authors and the Macmillan Company.

For assistance and advice, the author is especially indebted to

Mr. James L. Kelley of Alexandria, Virginia

Mr. William H. Price of Vienna, Virginia

Mr. James Small, Mr. Barney Friedland and Mr. Richard Patschke of Judd & Detweiler, Inc.

For assistance in preparing material for publication, he is indebted to Miss Brenda Hatmaker.

ABOUT THE AUTHOR

Historian, writer, editor, Mr. Wilson is also the author of *The Book of Distinguished American Women, The Book of the Founding Fathers* and *The Book of the States,* which was selected by the Freedoms Foundation at Valley Forge for its Honor Award. He is editor of *The Book of Great American Documents,* which was selected by the Freedoms Foundation in 1968 for its George Washington Honor Medal Award. A native of Cleveland, Mr. Wilson studied at Cleveland's University School and at Georgetown, Arizona State, Claremont and Harvard.